APPLY HYBRID APPROACH IMPLEMENTING PROJECT

TIPS AND TRICKS USING HYBRID | ADVANTAGES | DISADVANTAGES | CHALLENGES

ANGELA SIRBU, MBA. PMP

© 2024 by Angela Sirbu, MBA. PMP. All rights reserved.

No part of this book may be reproduced or utilized in any form or by any means, electronic or mechanical, including photocopying, recording, or by any information storage and retrieval system, without permission in writing from the publisher.

First Edition 2024

Published by Angela Sirbu, MBA. PMP

CONTENTS

INTRODUCTION

CHAPTER 1: INTRODUCTION TO HYBRID PROJECT MANAGEMENT

CHAPTER 2: FOUNDATIONS OF TRADITIONAL PROJECT MANAGEMENT

CHAPTER 3: FOUNDATIONS OF AGILE PROJECT MANAGEMENT

CHAPTER 4: INTEGRATING TRADITIONAL AND AGILE APPROACHES

CHAPTER 5: PLANNING IN A HYBRID ENVIRONMENT

CHAPTER 6: EXECUTING HYBRID PROJECTS

CHAPTER 7: LEADERSHIP IN HYBRID PROJECT MANAGEMENT

CHAPTER 8: COMMUNICATION STRATEGIES

CHAPTER 9: RISK MANAGEMENT IN HYBRID PROJECTS

CHAPTER 10: PERFORMANCE MEASUREMENT AND METRICS

CHAPTER 11: TECHNOLOGY AND TOOLS

CHAPTER 12: CASE STUDIES AND REAL-WORLD EXAMPLES

CHAPTER 13: ADVANTAGES AND DISADVANTAGES

CHAPTER 14: FUTURE OF HYBRID PROJECT MANAGEMENT

INTRODUCTION

In the dynamic world of project management, the quest for efficiency and effectiveness remains paramount. Traditional methodologies like Waterfall and Agile have long been the cornerstones of project execution, each offering distinct advantages and facing unique limitations. However, as the complexity and diversity of projects increase, a singular approach often proves inadequate. This evolving landscape has given rise to the Hybrid Approach, a versatile methodology that amalgamates the best practices of both Waterfall and Agile, tailored to meet the specific needs of each project.

"Apply Hybrid Approach Implementing Project" delves deep into this innovative strategy, designed for project managers, team leaders, and stakeholders who seek to optimize their project outcomes. This book offers a comprehensive exploration of the Hybrid Approach, presenting a balanced view of its practical applications, advantages, disadvantages, and the challenges one might encounter.

In the pages that follow, readers will discover a wealth of tips and tricks for effectively applying a Hybrid Approach, ensuring that projects are not only completed on time and within budget but also meet the desired quality standards. The book emphasizes the importance of flexibility, adaptability, and strategic planning, providing insights on how to seamlessly integrate the structured, sequential processes of Waterfall with the iterative, incremental benefits of Agile.

Moreover, this guide addresses the critical aspects of stakeholder management, team collaboration, and risk mitigation, all through the lens of a Hybrid Approach. By understanding the nuances of this methodology, project managers can better navigate the complexities of modern projects, fostering an environment where innovation and productivity thrive.

Whether you are a seasoned professional or new to the field of project management, this book serves as an invaluable resource. It equips you with the knowledge and tools necessary to harness the power of a Hybrid Approach, ultimately driving project success and delivering exceptional value to your organization.

Chapter 1: Introduction to Hybrid Project Management

Understanding Hybrid Approaches

Hybrid approaches in project management represent a confluence of methodologies designed to leverage the strengths of both traditional and agile frameworks. These methodologies aim to provide a more flexible, adaptive, and efficient strategy for managing projects in dynamic environments. The integration of diverse methodologies seeks to address the limitations inherent in using a single project management approach and to create a more versatile framework that can respond to varying project demands.

Traditional project management methodologies, such as Waterfall, are characterized by their linear and sequential nature. This approach is highly structured and relies on comprehensive upfront planning, where each phase must be completed before the next one begins. Waterfall is particularly effective in projects with well-defined requirements and minimal expected changes. However, it often struggles in environments where requirements are likely to evolve, leading to potential inefficiencies and delays.

Conversely, agile methodologies prioritize iterative progress, flexibility, and customer collaboration. Agile frameworks, such as Scrum and Kanban, are designed to accommodate changing requirements and to deliver incremental value through continuous feedback and iterative cycles. Agile is particularly advantageous in projects where uncertainty is high, and adaptability is crucial. Despite its strengths, agile can sometimes lack the formal structure needed for complex projects with stringent regulatory or compliance requirements.

The hybrid approach synthesizes elements from both traditional and agile methodologies to create a tailored project management strategy. This synthesis allows project managers to benefit from the structured planning and risk management of traditional methods while also taking advantage of the adaptability and iterative progress inherent in agile frameworks. The hybrid approach is especially useful in projects where different phases may require different management styles. For instance, the initial phases of a project may benefit from the detailed planning and risk assessment typical of traditional methodologies, while later phases may require the flexibility and rapid iteration provided by agile practices.

Implementing a hybrid approach necessitates a thorough understanding of the project's context, including its complexity, stakeholder requirements, and potential risks. Project managers must be adept at identifying which elements of traditional and agile methodologies are most pertinent to each phase of the project. This requires a deep knowledge of both frameworks and the ability to seamlessly integrate them to suit the project's unique needs.

A critical aspect of the hybrid approach is the ability to foster effective communication and collaboration among team members. Since hybrid projects may involve a mix of different methodologies, it is essential to ensure that all team members understand the chosen approach and are aligned with its objectives. This alignment can be achieved through regular meetings, transparent communication channels, and a shared understanding of project goals and deliverables.

Moreover, the hybrid approach often necessitates a cultural shift within the organization. Teams must be willing to adopt a more flexible mindset, embrace change, and prioritize continuous improvement. This cultural shift can be facilitated through training programs, leadership support, and the establishment of a supportive environment that encourages experimentation and innovation.

Incorporating a hybrid approach in project management also involves leveraging appropriate tools and technologies. These tools can help streamline processes, enhance collaboration, and provide real-time insights into project progress. Selecting the right tools is crucial for effectively managing the diverse aspects of hybrid projects and ensuring that all team members are equipped to contribute to the project's success.

The hybrid approach represents a strategic evolution in project management, offering a versatile and adaptive framework capable of addressing the multifaceted challenges of modern projects. By combining the strengths of traditional and agile methodologies, the hybrid approach provides a comprehensive strategy that can enhance project outcomes and drive organizational success.

Historical Context and Evolution

The development and application of hybrid project management methodologies have evolved significantly over time. Initially, project management was dominated by traditional approaches such as Waterfall, which emphasized a linear, sequential progression through project phases. This method, characterized by its rigidity and detailed upfront planning, was well-suited for projects with well-defined requirements and minimal expected changes. However, as industries and technologies evolved, the limitations of traditional methodologies became increasingly apparent, particularly in environments characterized by rapid change and uncertainty.

The emergence of Agile methodologies in the early 2000s marked a significant shift in project management practices. Agile, with its iterative and incremental approach, offered a more flexible and adaptive framework. It emphasized collaboration, customer feedback, and the ability to respond to change, which made it particularly effective in software development and other dynamic fields. The Agile Manifesto, published in 2001, outlined the core values and principles that would guide this new approach, emphasizing individuals and interactions over processes and tools, working software over comprehensive documentation, customer collaboration over contract negotiation, and responding to change over following a plan.

As Agile gained popularity, many organizations began to recognize the potential benefits of integrating Agile principles with their existing traditional project management practices. This integration led to the development of hybrid project management methodologies, which combine elements of both traditional and Agile approaches to leverage their respective strengths. Hybrid methodologies aim to provide the structured planning and control of traditional methods while also incorporating the flexibility and responsiveness of Agile practices.

One of the key drivers behind the adoption of hybrid methodologies is the need to address the diverse and evolving requirements of modern projects. Different industries and project types often necessitate varying degrees of flexibility and control. Hybrid approaches allow organizations to tailor their project management practices to better align with specific project needs, stakeholder expectations, and organizational goals. For example, a hybrid approach might involve using traditional methods for the initial planning and design phases of a project, followed by Agile techniques for implementation and testing.

Another important factor contributing to the rise of hybrid methodologies is the increasing complexity of projects. As projects become more multifaceted, involving multiple teams, stakeholders, and technologies, a one-size-fits-all approach to project management becomes less effective. Hybrid methodologies provide a more nuanced and adaptable framework that can accommodate the unique challenges and requirements of complex projects.

The evolution of hybrid project management is also influenced by advancements in tools and technologies. Modern project management software and collaboration platforms enable teams to seamlessly integrate traditional and Agile practices, providing real-time visibility and control over project progress. These tools facilitate communication, coordination, and decision-making, which are critical for the successful implementation of hybrid methodologies.

In addition, the growing emphasis on continuous improvement and learning within organizations has driven the adoption of hybrid approaches. By combining traditional and Agile practices, organizations can create a more balanced and iterative process that supports ongoing refinement and optimization. This continuous improvement mindset is essential for maintaining competitiveness and achieving long-term success in today's fast-paced and ever-changing business environment.

The historical context and evolution of hybrid project management methodologies reflect a broader trend towards greater flexibility, adaptability, and integration in project management practices. As organizations continue to navigate the complexities of modern projects, the hybrid approach offers a versatile and effective framework that can meet the diverse needs of various industries and project types.

Benefits of Hybrid Project Management

Hybrid project management methodologies integrate the strengths of traditional and agile project management approaches. This synthesis allows organizations to benefit from the structured, sequential processes of traditional methods while simultaneously leveraging the adaptability and responsiveness of agile techniques. These hybrid methodologies offer several advantages that can lead to more successful project outcomes.

One significant benefit is enhanced flexibility. Traditional project management methodologies, such as Waterfall, follow a linear and sequential approach, which can be rigid and less adaptable to changes once the project is underway. In contrast, agile methodologies are iterative and incremental, allowing for adjustments based on ongoing feedback and changes in project requirements. By combining these approaches, hybrid project management provides a framework that can adapt to changes more effectively, ensuring that projects remain aligned with evolving business needs and stakeholder expectations.

Another advantage is improved risk management. Hybrid methodologies enable project managers to identify potential risks early in the project lifecycle and address them proactively. The structured planning phase of traditional methods allows for comprehensive risk assessment and mitigation strategies, while the iterative nature of agile allows for continuous monitoring and adaptation to new risks as they emerge. This dual-layered approach helps in managing uncertainties more effectively, reducing the likelihood of project failures.

Resource optimization is also a notable benefit of hybrid project management. By integrating agile practices, teams can break down large, complex projects into smaller, manageable tasks. This facilitates better allocation of resources, as team members can focus on specific tasks within shorter time frames, leading to increased productivity and efficiency. Additionally, the structured nature of traditional methods ensures that resources are allocated systematically, avoiding the pitfalls of over- or under-utilization.

Hybrid project management also fosters better stakeholder engagement and communication. Traditional methods often emphasize detailed documentation and formal communication channels, which can ensure clarity and accountability. Agile methodologies, on the other hand, prioritize continuous collaboration and feedback through regular meetings and updates. Combining these practices allows for a balanced approach where stakeholders are kept informed and engaged throughout the project lifecycle, facilitating better decision-making and stakeholder satisfaction.

The ability to deliver higher-quality outcomes is another benefit of hybrid project management. The iterative cycles of agile methodologies incorporate regular testing and validation stages, allowing for early detection and correction of defects. This continuous quality assurance process, coupled with the thorough planning and documentation of traditional methods, ensures that the final deliverable meets or exceeds quality standards. This hybrid approach can lead to more robust and reliable project outcomes.

Scalability is an additional advantage offered by hybrid project management. Traditional methodologies are well-suited for large-scale projects with clearly defined scopes and long timelines, while agile methodologies excel in smaller, fast-paced environments with evolving requirements. By adopting a hybrid approach, organizations can tailor their project management practices to suit the scale and complexity of each project, ensuring that they can effectively manage both small and large initiatives.

Incorporating hybrid project management methodologies can also lead to improved team dynamics and morale. Agile practices emphasize collaborative work environments and empower team members to take ownership of their tasks, fostering a sense of autonomy and motivation. The clear roles and responsibilities defined by traditional methods provide structure and reduce ambiguity, contributing to a more organized and cohesive team dynamic. This blend of autonomy and structure can enhance team performance and satisfaction.

Incorporating the strengths of both traditional and agile methodologies, hybrid project management offers a comprehensive approach that can address the diverse needs of modern projects. Enhanced flexibility, improved risk management, resource optimization, better stakeholder engagement, higher quality outcomes, scalability, and improved team dynamics are among the key benefits that make hybrid project management a valuable strategy for organizations aiming to achieve successful project delivery.

Challenges in Hybrid Project Management

Implementing a hybrid approach in project management introduces a unique set of challenges, given the necessity to integrate methodologies that often have fundamentally different principles and practices. These challenges can be broadly categorized into cultural, procedural, and technical domains.

Cultural challenges emerge primarily from the need to align diverse mindsets and work ethics. Traditional project management methodologies, such as Waterfall, emphasize a structured, sequential approach, while Agile methodologies focus on iterative development and flexibility. Project teams accustomed to one methodology may exhibit resistance to change, leading to conflicts and decreased morale. Overcoming these cultural barriers requires robust change management practices, including comprehensive training programs, continuous communication, and fostering an environment that values adaptability and collaboration.

Procedural challenges involve the harmonization of different project management processes and practices. Hybrid project management necessitates the integration of structured planning and documentation from traditional methodologies with the adaptive and iterative cycles characteristic of Agile frameworks. This integration can lead to complexity in project planning, execution, and monitoring. Establishing a coherent framework that delineates clear guidelines for when and how to apply different methodologies within the hybrid model is crucial. Additionally, maintaining consistency in reporting and performance metrics is essential to ensure that stakeholders have a clear and unified understanding of project progress and outcomes.

Technical challenges are associated with the tools and technologies employed to support hybrid project management. The selection of appropriate project management software that can accommodate both traditional and Agile practices is critical. Many existing tools are specialized for either Waterfall or Agile methodologies, and finding or customizing a tool that effectively bridges this gap can be difficult. Furthermore, the integration of these tools with other enterprise systems, such as resource management and financial tracking software, adds another layer of complexity. Ensuring seamless data flow and interoperability between different systems is essential to avoid disruptions and inefficiencies.

Another significant challenge is the alignment of stakeholder expectations. Stakeholders, including clients, sponsors, and team members, may have varying degrees of familiarity and comfort with hybrid methodologies. Clear and transparent communication is vital to manage expectations and ensure that all parties understand the hybrid approach's benefits and limitations. Regular updates, demonstrations, and feedback loops can help in aligning stakeholder expectations and fostering a collaborative environment.

Resource management is also a critical challenge in hybrid project management. The need to allocate resources efficiently across different phases and methodologies requires meticulous planning and foresight. Balancing the workload between teams operating under different methodologies can be difficult, particularly when transitioning from one phase to another. Effective resource management strategies, such as cross-training team members and implementing flexible resource allocation models, can mitigate these challenges.

Finally, ensuring continuous improvement and learning within the hybrid framework is essential. Given the dynamic nature of hybrid project management, regular retrospectives and reviews should be conducted to identify areas for improvement and to adapt practices accordingly. This iterative learning process helps in refining the hybrid approach and in addressing emerging challenges proactively.

In summary, while hybrid project management offers the flexibility to leverage the strengths of multiple methodologies, it also presents a complex array of challenges. Addressing these challenges requires a thoughtful and strategic approach, encompassing cultural alignment, procedural integration, technical support, stakeholder management, resource optimization, and continuous learning. By navigating these challenges effectively, organizations can harness the full potential of hybrid project management to achieve enhanced project outcomes.

Chapter 2: Foundations of Traditional Project Management

Core Principles

Hybrid project management represents a confluence of traditional and agile methodologies, tailored to leverage the strengths of both approaches. This fusion aims to enhance flexibility, responsiveness, and efficiency in project execution. The core principles underpinning this approach are essential for understanding its application and potential benefits.

First, stakeholder engagement and communication are paramount. In hybrid project management, stakeholders' needs and expectations must be continuously assessed and integrated into the project lifecycle. This requires transparent, iterative communication channels that facilitate feedback and adjustments. Effective stakeholder engagement ensures alignment with project goals and fosters a collaborative environment, crucial for the successful implementation of hybrid methodologies.

Second, the principle of adaptability is central to hybrid project management. This approach necessitates a dynamic framework that can accommodate changes in scope, requirements, and external conditions. Adaptability is achieved through iterative planning and review cycles, which allow project teams to pivot and reallocate resources as needed. This continuous reassessment and adjustment process is essential for maintaining project momentum and achieving desired outcomes.

Third, risk management is a critical component of hybrid project management. Identifying, assessing, and mitigating risks at various stages of the project lifecycle is vital. This involves integrating risk management practices from both traditional and agile frameworks. Traditional risk management techniques, such as risk registers and mitigation plans, are combined with agile practices like regular risk reviews and adaptive responses. This dual approach enhances the project's resilience to uncertainties and potential disruptions.

Fourth, a balanced approach to documentation and process rigor is necessary. Hybrid project management requires a judicious blend of formal documentation and agile flexibility. While comprehensive documentation ensures clarity and traceability, excessive paperwork can hinder agility. Therefore, the project team must strike a balance, maintaining essential documentation without compromising the ability to respond swiftly to changes.

Fifth, resource optimization is a fundamental principle. Efficient allocation and utilization of resources, including human capital, technology, and finances, are crucial for project success. Hybrid project management leverages resource management techniques from both traditional and agile methodologies. This includes detailed resource planning and adaptive resource allocation, ensuring that resources are deployed effectively throughout the project lifecycle.

Sixth, continuous improvement is embedded in the hybrid approach. This principle emphasizes the importance of learning and refining processes. Regular retrospectives and performance reviews are conducted to identify areas for improvement. This iterative process of reflection and enhancement fosters a culture of continuous improvement, driving project teams towards higher levels of efficiency and effectiveness.

Seventh, the alignment of project objectives with organizational strategy is essential. Hybrid project management requires that project goals are consistently aligned with broader organizational objectives. This alignment ensures that the project contributes to the strategic aims of the organization, enhancing its overall value and impact.

Eighth, the principle of team empowerment and collaboration is vital. Hybrid methodologies advocate for empowered, cross-functional teams that have the autonomy to make decisions and adapt processes. This empowerment fosters a sense of ownership and accountability, leading to higher levels of team engagement and productivity.

Lastly, the integration of technology and tools is a key principle. Leveraging appropriate project management software and tools facilitates the seamless execution of hybrid methodologies. These tools support various functions, including project planning, tracking, communication, and reporting, thereby enhancing the efficiency and effectiveness of project management activities.

By adhering to these core principles, organizations can effectively implement hybrid project management, harnessing the benefits of both traditional and agile approaches to achieve successful project outcomes.

Key Methodologies

Hybrid project management integrates traditional and agile methodologies to leverage the strengths of both approaches. This chapter examines key methodologies essential for implementing a hybrid approach effectively.

Waterfall methodology serves as the backbone of many traditional project management frameworks. Characterized by its linear and sequential phases, it includes distinct stages such as initiation, planning, execution, monitoring, and closure. The clarity and structure of the Waterfall model make it particularly suitable for projects with well-defined requirements and deliverables. However, its rigidity can pose challenges in dynamic environments where requirements may evolve.

Agile methodology, on the other hand, offers flexibility and adaptability, which are critical in rapidly changing project landscapes. Agile emphasizes iterative progress through small, manageable increments known as sprints or iterations. Each iteration involves planning, execution, and review, allowing for frequent reassessment and adjustment of project goals. Agile methodologies like Scrum and Kanban are widely used due to their ability to accommodate changing requirements and foster continuous improvement.

Scrum, a popular Agile framework, organizes work into time-boxed iterations called sprints, usually lasting two to four weeks. Scrum emphasizes roles such as the Product Owner, Scrum Master, and Development Team, each with specific responsibilities. The Product Owner prioritizes the backlog, ensuring the team focuses on the most critical tasks. The Scrum Master facilitates the process, removing obstacles and ensuring adherence to Scrum practices. Daily stand-up meetings, sprint planning, sprint review, and sprint retrospective meetings enable continuous feedback and improvement.

Kanban, another Agile methodology, focuses on visualizing work, limiting work in progress, and maximizing flow efficiency. Kanban boards display tasks in columns representing different stages of the workflow, such as "To Do," "In Progress," and "Done." Teams can quickly identify bottlenecks and inefficiencies, making it easier to optimize processes. Unlike Scrum, Kanban does not prescribe specific roles or time-boxed iterations, offering more flexibility in managing work.

Integrating Waterfall and Agile methodologies requires a nuanced approach to balance structure and flexibility. One effective strategy is to use Waterfall for the overall project framework while incorporating Agile practices within specific phases or components. For example, the initial planning and design stages can follow the Waterfall model to establish a clear project roadmap. Subsequent development and testing phases can adopt Agile practices, allowing for iterative progress and continuous feedback.

Another approach involves using a hybrid framework like Disciplined Agile Delivery (DAD) or the Scaled Agile Framework (SAFe). DAD provides a process decision framework that guides teams in choosing the most appropriate practices based on the project's context. It combines elements from Scrum, Kanban, Lean, and traditional methodologies, offering a customizable approach to project management. SAFe, designed for large-scale projects, integrates Lean and Agile principles with traditional management practices. It provides a structured approach to scaling Agile across multiple teams and departments, ensuring alignment with organizational goals.

Effective communication and collaboration are vital for successful hybrid project management. Regular meetings, transparent reporting, and stakeholder engagement ensure alignment and address potential issues promptly. Tools like JIRA, Trello, and Microsoft Project can facilitate task management and collaboration, providing real-time visibility into project progress.

Implementing a hybrid approach requires a deep understanding of both Waterfall and Agile methodologies, as well as the ability to adapt and integrate these practices based on project needs. By leveraging the strengths of each methodology, project managers can navigate complex projects with greater agility and precision.

Strengths of Traditional Approaches

Traditional project management methodologies, such as Waterfall and Critical Path Method (CPM), have been foundational in the field of project management for decades. These methodologies offer several strengths that have contributed to their widespread adoption and persistent relevance. One of the primary advantages of traditional approaches is their structured and sequential nature. This structure allows for clear, linear progression through project phases, which facilitates meticulous planning and scheduling. By defining distinct phases such as initiation, planning, execution, monitoring and controlling, and closing, traditional methodologies provide a comprehensive framework that ensures all critical aspects of the project are addressed systematically.

The predictability and control offered by traditional methodologies are crucial in industries where regulatory compliance and risk management are paramount. For instance, in construction and manufacturing, adherence to detailed plans and schedules is essential to meet stringent safety and quality standards. The Waterfall model, with its emphasis on upfront planning and design, helps in minimizing uncertainties by ensuring that each phase is thoroughly completed before moving on to the next. This reduces the risk of costly rework and scope creep, thereby enhancing the predictability of project outcomes.

Another significant strength of traditional project management approaches is their emphasis on documentation and formalization. Detailed documentation, including project plans, schedules, and progress reports, provides a clear and comprehensive record of the project's trajectory. This documentation is invaluable for stakeholders who require transparency and accountability. The ability to refer to well-documented plans and progress reports aids in maintaining alignment among team members and stakeholders, thereby fostering effective communication and collaboration.

Resource management is another area where traditional approaches excel. The Critical Path Method (CPM), for example, enables project managers to identify the most crucial tasks that directly impact the project's completion date. By focusing on these critical tasks, project managers can allocate resources more efficiently and prioritize activities that are vital to the project's success. This methodical allocation of resources ensures that projects are completed within the specified timeframes and budgets, thereby enhancing overall project efficiency.

Traditional methodologies also offer the benefit of well-established best practices and standards. Over the years, these methodologies have been refined and standardized, resulting in a wealth of knowledge and expertise that project managers can draw upon. The Project Management Institute's (PMI) Project Management Body of Knowledge (PMBOK) serves as a comprehensive guide that encapsulates these best practices. The availability of such standardized guidelines aids in the consistent application of project management principles across different projects and industries.

Moreover, traditional approaches are particularly effective in projects with well-defined requirements and stable environments. In such contexts, the upfront investment in detailed planning and design pays off by providing a clear roadmap for project execution. This clarity is especially beneficial in large-scale projects where coordination among multiple teams and stakeholders is essential. The predefined milestones and deliverables in traditional methodologies facilitate progress tracking and ensure that the project remains on course.

While the rigidity of traditional methodologies may be seen as a limitation in dynamic and rapidly changing environments, their strengths in predictability, control, documentation, resource management, and adherence to best practices make them indispensable in many project contexts. These strengths underscore the enduring value of traditional project management approaches, even as organizations increasingly explore hybrid methodologies to address the complexities of modern projects.

Limitations and Drawbacks

Implementing a hybrid approach in project management presents several limitations and drawbacks that necessitate careful consideration. One primary concern is the complexity involved in integrating different methodologies. Hybrid approaches often require combining elements from traditional Waterfall and Agile frameworks, which can lead to confusion and inconsistency in execution. Teams may struggle to adapt to the varying demands of each method, potentially undermining productivity and cohesion.

Another significant issue is the potential for communication breakdowns. Hybrid methodologies often involve diverse teams with different working styles and expectations. Ensuring seamless communication across these groups can be challenging, particularly when team members are accustomed to distinct terminologies and processes. This can result in misunderstandings, delays, and errors, ultimately compromising project outcomes.

Resource allocation is another critical challenge. Hybrid approaches frequently demand varied skill sets and expertise, which can strain available resources. Allocating the right personnel to the right tasks becomes more complex, and there is a risk of overburdening team members with conflicting responsibilities. This can lead to burnout and reduced morale, further impacting project performance.

The learning curve associated with hybrid methodologies cannot be overlooked. Teams and managers must invest significant time and effort in understanding and mastering the integrated approach. This learning phase can delay project initiation and progress, as well as increase the likelihood of mistakes during the early stages of implementation. Organizations must be prepared to provide adequate training and support to mitigate this issue.

Moreover, the flexibility of hybrid approaches, while beneficial in many respects, can also be a double-edged sword. Excessive flexibility may lead to a lack of clear direction and focus, causing teams to veer off course. Without stringent oversight and control mechanisms, projects can easily become disorganized, resulting in missed deadlines and budget overruns.

Another drawback is the potential resistance to change. Teams accustomed to a single methodology may be reluctant to adopt a hybrid approach, viewing it as an unnecessary complication. Overcoming this resistance requires effective change management strategies, which can be time-consuming and resource-intensive. Failure to address these concerns can lead to a lack of buy-in and commitment from team members, adversely affecting project success.

The integration of tools and software also poses a challenge. Hybrid approaches often necessitate the use of multiple project management tools, each tailored to different methodologies. Ensuring compatibility and seamless integration between these tools can be technically demanding and costly. Incompatibilities can lead to data silos and inefficiencies, further complicating project management efforts.

Additionally, measuring performance and success in a hybrid environment can be problematic. Traditional metrics may not apply, and new performance indicators must be developed to accurately assess progress and outcomes. This requires a thorough understanding of both methodologies and their respective metrics, adding to the complexity of the approach.

Finally, the scalability of hybrid methodologies is a concern. While they may work well for small to medium-sized projects, scaling up to larger initiatives can be challenging. The intricacies of managing a hybrid approach on a large scale can lead to increased risks and uncertainties, necessitating robust risk management strategies.

In conclusion, while hybrid approaches offer numerous benefits, they also come with significant limitations and drawbacks. Organizations must carefully weigh these factors and implement appropriate strategies to address the associated challenges.

Chapter 3: Foundations of Agile Project Management

Agile Principles and Values

The Agile methodology has emerged as a pivotal framework in project management, emphasizing flexibility, collaboration, and customer satisfaction. Central to this methodology are its core principles and values, which serve as the foundation for its successful implementation. These principles and values are encapsulated within the Agile Manifesto, a document formulated by seventeen software developers in 2001, which underscores the importance of individuals and interactions, working software, customer collaboration, and responding to change.

At the heart of Agile is the prioritization of individuals and interactions over processes and tools. This principle posits that the success of a project is largely dependent on the people involved and their ability to communicate and collaborate effectively. In contrast to traditional project management approaches that often emphasize rigid processes and standardized tools, Agile advocates for a more human-centric approach. This shift in focus facilitates adaptability and innovation, fostering an environment where team members can respond dynamically to evolving project requirements.

The second principle emphasizes the delivery of working software over comprehensive documentation. While documentation remains an important aspect of project management, Agile stresses the importance of producing tangible, functional outputs that can be evaluated and utilized by stakeholders. This approach not only accelerates the feedback loop but also ensures that the project's progress is aligned with the client's needs and expectations. By delivering incremental, functional components of the project, teams can gather valuable insights and make informed adjustments, thereby enhancing the overall quality and relevance of the final product.

Customer collaboration is another cornerstone of Agile methodology. This principle advocates for continuous engagement with customers throughout the project lifecycle, as opposed to a one-time negotiation at the project's inception. Regular interactions with customers allow for the incorporation of their feedback and evolving requirements, ensuring that the end product is closely aligned with their expectations. This collaborative approach mitigates the risks associated with miscommunication and misalignment, which are common pitfalls in traditional project management.

The fourth principle, responding to change over following a plan, encapsulates the Agile philosophy of flexibility and adaptability. In a rapidly changing business environment, the ability to pivot and adjust to new information and circumstances is crucial. Agile methodology recognizes that initial plans may become obsolete or irrelevant as the project progresses. Therefore, it encourages teams to remain open to change and to view it as an opportunity for improvement rather than a disruption. This principle is particularly relevant in the context of hybrid project management, where the integration of Agile with other methodologies necessitates a high degree of adaptability.

Underlying these principles are the values that the Agile Manifesto promotes: communication, simplicity, feedback, and courage. Effective communication is essential for fostering collaboration and ensuring that all team members are aligned with the project's goals. Simplicity, on the other hand, is about maximizing the amount of work not done, thereby focusing on what truly adds value. Feedback is integral to the iterative process, enabling continuous improvement and refinement. Lastly, courage is required to embrace change, take risks, and make difficult decisions in the face of uncertainty.

The principles and values of Agile methodology offer a robust framework for managing projects in a dynamic environment. By emphasizing flexibility, collaboration, and customer-centricity, Agile provides a pathway for delivering high-quality outcomes that meet the evolving needs of stakeholders.

Agile Frameworks and Practices

Hybrid project management approaches integrate elements from various methodologies to tailor solutions that best fit specific project requirements. Agile frameworks and practices are pivotal in this integration, providing flexible, iterative processes that enhance responsiveness and adaptability.

Scrum, one of the most widely recognized Agile frameworks, emphasizes iterative progress through sprints, typically lasting two to four weeks. Each sprint culminates in a potentially shippable product increment. Scrum roles, including the Product Owner, Scrum Master, and Development Team, ensure clear responsibilities and foster collaboration. Scrum ceremonies, such as Sprint Planning, Daily Stand-ups, Sprint Reviews, and Retrospectives, structure the workflow and promote continuous improvement.

Kanban, another Agile methodology, focuses on visualizing the workflow and limiting work in progress to enhance efficiency. By using a Kanban board, teams can monitor the flow of tasks through various stages, identifying bottlenecks and optimizing processes. Kanban's principles, including managing flow, making process policies explicit, and implementing feedback loops, support incremental and evolutionary change.

Lean software development, originating from Lean manufacturing principles, aims to eliminate waste and deliver value efficiently. Lean practices include value stream mapping, which identifies and removes non-value-adding activities, and continuous integration, which ensures frequent, automated testing and integration of code. Lean principles, such as delivering fast by managing flow and empowering teams, align closely with Agile values.

Extreme Programming (XP) emphasizes technical excellence and customer satisfaction through practices like pair programming, test-driven development, and continuous integration. XP advocates for frequent releases in short development cycles, which improves productivity and introduces checkpoints for new customer requirements. The focus on code quality and frequent feedback loops enhances the reliability and functionality of the final product.

The Scaled Agile Framework (SAFe) addresses the need for scaling Agile practices across large enterprises. SAFe integrates Lean, Agile, and DevOps principles, providing a structured approach to scaling Agile methods. Key components of SAFe include Agile Release Trains, which synchronize the work of multiple teams, and Program Increments, which align team efforts with business objectives over a fixed timeframe. SAFe's emphasis on alignment, built-in quality, and transparency enables organizations to scale Agile practices while maintaining coherence and control.

Agile practices extend beyond specific frameworks, encompassing techniques that enhance collaboration and productivity. User stories and story mapping help teams understand customer needs and prioritize work based on value. Continuous integration and continuous delivery (CI/CD) pipelines automate testing and deployment, reducing the time between code changes and production releases. Agile metrics, such as velocity, lead time, and cycle time, provide insights into team performance and process efficiency.

Incorporating Agile frameworks and practices into a hybrid project management approach requires careful consideration of the project context and objectives. Hybrid models often combine Agile methods with traditional project management techniques, such as the Waterfall model, to balance flexibility with structure. For example, a project might use Scrum for software development while employing Waterfall for hardware components, ensuring that each aspect of the project benefits from the most suitable methodology.

The integration of Agile frameworks and practices into hybrid approaches necessitates a cultural shift towards collaboration, transparency, and continuous improvement. Organizations must foster an environment that supports Agile values and principles, encouraging teams to experiment, learn, and adapt. By leveraging the strengths of both Agile and traditional methodologies, hybrid approaches can effectively address complex project requirements, driving innovation and delivering value.

Strengths of Agile Approaches

Agile methodologies, characterized by iterative development, collaboration, and flexibility, have garnered substantial attention for their efficacy in managing modern projects. One of the primary strengths of Agile approaches is their ability to adapt to changing requirements and environments. Traditional project management methodologies, such as Waterfall, often struggle with accommodating changes once a project is underway. In contrast, Agile frameworks like Scrum and Kanban are designed to be inherently adaptive, allowing teams to respond to feedback and evolving needs promptly.

The iterative nature of Agile promotes continuous improvement and innovation. By breaking down projects into smaller, manageable increments known as sprints or iterations, teams can focus on delivering functional components of a project at regular intervals. This not only ensures that progress is visible and measurable but also allows for frequent reassessment and realignment of project goals and priorities. Stakeholders can review the deliverables at the end of each iteration and provide feedback, which can be incorporated into subsequent iterations. This feedback loop enhances the quality and relevance of the final product.

Collaboration is a cornerstone of Agile methodologies. Agile frameworks emphasize cross-functional teams where members from different disciplines work closely together throughout the project lifecycle. This collaborative environment fosters better communication, reduces misunderstandings, and ensures that all team members are aligned with the project goals. Daily stand-up meetings, a common practice in Agile, facilitate transparency and allow team members to share progress, identify obstacles, and coordinate efforts efficiently. This level of collaboration ensures that issues are addressed promptly, and solutions are devised collectively, leveraging the diverse expertise within the team.

Agile approaches also prioritize customer satisfaction by involving stakeholders throughout the project. Regular interactions with stakeholders, including customers, ensure that their needs and expectations are understood and met. This ongoing engagement helps in building trust and ensures that the project remains aligned with the stakeholders' vision. Moreover, by delivering working increments of the product early and often, Agile teams can provide tangible value to customers sooner, which can be critical in fast-paced and competitive markets.

Risk management is another area where Agile methodologies excel. The iterative approach allows for early detection and mitigation of risks. By focusing on delivering smaller increments, potential issues can be identified and addressed before they escalate into larger problems. This proactive approach to risk management enhances the overall resilience of the project and contributes to its success.

Agile methodologies also promote a culture of accountability and ownership. Team members are empowered to make decisions and take responsibility for their tasks, which fosters a sense of ownership and commitment. This empowerment leads to higher morale and motivation, as team members feel more valued and engaged in the project's success.

Incorporating Agile approaches into a hybrid project management framework can leverage these strengths while also benefiting from the structured planning and control mechanisms of traditional methodologies. This hybrid approach can provide a balanced and flexible strategy that is well-suited to the complexities and uncertainties of contemporary projects.

Limitations and Challenges

The hybrid approach to project implementation, which integrates both traditional and agile methodologies, offers several advantages such as enhanced flexibility, improved stakeholder engagement, and optimized resource allocation. However, this approach is not without its limitations and challenges, which must be critically examined to ensure successful project outcomes.

A critical limitation of the hybrid approach lies in the complexity of its implementation. The necessity to blend two distinct methodologies demands a comprehensive understanding of both traditional and agile frameworks. Project managers must be adept at recognizing when to apply specific principles from each methodology, which can be a daunting task, especially in large-scale projects with multifaceted requirements. This complexity is further exacerbated by the need for continuous adjustments and fine-tuning to maintain the balance between flexibility and control.

Another significant challenge is the potential for resistance to change within the organization. Stakeholders and team members accustomed to a single methodology may exhibit reluctance to adopt a hybrid approach. This resistance can stem from a lack of understanding, fear of the unknown, or a preference for familiar processes. Overcoming this resistance requires effective change management strategies, including comprehensive training programs, clear communication of the benefits, and the involvement of key stakeholders in the transition process.

Resource allocation and management also pose considerable challenges in a hybrid project environment. Balancing resources between agile and traditional tasks necessitates meticulous planning and constant monitoring. The dynamic nature of agile methodologies can lead to fluctuating resource demands, which can strain the project's resource pool if not managed effectively. Additionally, the duality of the approach may result in conflicting priorities, making it difficult to allocate resources optimally without compromising on project deliverables.

The integration of disparate tools and technologies required by each methodology presents another hurdle. Traditional project management often relies on well-established tools for scheduling, budgeting, and reporting, while agile methodologies favor tools that support iterative development and continuous feedback. Ensuring seamless interoperability between these tools is crucial to maintain coherence in project tracking and reporting. Failure to achieve this integration can lead to data silos, inconsistent information, and ultimately, project inefficiencies.

Maintaining team cohesion and communication in a hybrid environment is also challenging. Agile methodologies emphasize collaboration and frequent communication, often through daily stand-ups and iterative reviews. In contrast, traditional methodologies may rely on formal, periodic reporting. Striking a balance between these communication styles to foster effective collaboration without overwhelming team members with meetings and reports is essential. Misalignment in communication practices can lead to misunderstandings, reduced morale, and decreased productivity.

Finally, the hybrid approach demands a high level of adaptability from project managers and teams. The ability to pivot between methodologies based on project needs requires not only technical proficiency but also a mindset geared towards continuous improvement and learning. This adaptability can be hindered by rigid organizational structures, a lack of support from leadership, or inadequate training programs.

In conclusion, while the hybrid approach to project implementation offers numerous benefits, its limitations and challenges are significant and must be addressed proactively. Success in a hybrid environment hinges on the ability to manage complexity, overcome resistance to change, allocate resources effectively, integrate tools seamlessly, maintain team cohesion, and foster adaptability. By recognizing and addressing these challenges, organizations can better leverage the strengths of both traditional and agile methodologies to achieve their project goals.

Chapter 4: Integrating Traditional and Agile Approaches

Identifying Compatibility

The integration of hybrid methodologies in project management necessitates a meticulous evaluation of compatibility between traditional and agile approaches. This assessment is fundamental to ensure that the hybrid model aligns with the unique requirements and constraints of the project. A comprehensive understanding of the project's scope, objectives, and environment is crucial to identify the most suitable hybrid approach.

The initial step involves a detailed analysis of the project's characteristics. Projects vary widely in terms of complexity, duration, stakeholder involvement, and deliverables. Traditional methodologies, such as Waterfall, are linear and sequential, making them suitable for projects with well-defined stages and clear requirements. Conversely, agile methodologies, such as Scrum or Kanban, are iterative and flexible, accommodating changes and fostering continuous improvement. The choice between these methodologies, or a combination thereof, hinges on the specific demands of the project.

Stakeholder analysis is another critical component in determining compatibility. Stakeholders, including clients, team members, and sponsors, have varying expectations and levels of involvement. Traditional approaches often require comprehensive documentation and upfront planning, which can be reassuring for stakeholders who prefer predictability and detailed plans. Agile approaches, on the other hand, emphasize collaboration and adaptability, appealing to stakeholders who value responsiveness and iterative progress. Understanding stakeholder preferences and expectations can guide the selection of a hybrid approach that balances these needs.

Risk assessment is integral in identifying compatibility. Projects inherently involve risks, and the management of these risks can differ significantly between methodologies. Traditional methods typically incorporate extensive risk management plans developed during the initial phases of the project. Agile methods, however, manage risks through iterative cycles and constant feedback, allowing for adjustments as the project progresses. Evaluating the project's risk profile and determining the most effective risk management strategy is essential in selecting a compatible hybrid approach.

Resource availability and allocation also influence the choice of methodology. Traditional approaches often require significant upfront resource allocation for planning and design phases, while agile methods distribute resources more evenly throughout the project lifecycle. Assessing the availability of resources, including personnel, budget, and technology, is necessary to ensure the chosen hybrid approach is feasible and sustainable.

Organizational culture and maturity play a pivotal role in the successful implementation of a hybrid approach. Organizations with a history of traditional project management may find it challenging to adopt agile practices without adequate training and mindset shifts. Conversely, organizations with an agile background may struggle with the rigidity of traditional methods. Evaluating the organization's readiness for change and its capacity to support a hybrid model is crucial for compatibility.

The assessment of tools and technologies is also vital. Hybrid approaches often require the integration of various project management tools to support both traditional and agile practices. Tools such as Gantt charts, which are prevalent in traditional methodologies, need to be complemented with agile tools like burndown charts and Kanban boards. Ensuring that the organization has access to, and proficiency with, these tools is key to the successful implementation of a hybrid approach.

In-depth evaluation of these factors facilitates the identification of a compatible hybrid approach tailored to the project's specific needs. This assessment ensures that the chosen methodology enhances efficiency, mitigates risks, and aligns with stakeholder expectations, ultimately contributing to the successful execution of the project.

Frameworks for Integration

Hybrid project management approaches combine traditional and agile methodologies to leverage the strengths of both frameworks, optimizing project outcomes. Various frameworks facilitate the integration of these methodologies, each offering distinct advantages and considerations that cater to different project requirements and organizational contexts.

One prominent framework is the Disciplined Agile Delivery (DAD) framework, which provides a comprehensive approach to hybrid project management. DAD extends agile methodologies by incorporating traditional project management practices, ensuring a structured yet flexible approach to project delivery. It emphasizes the importance of context-specific strategies, enabling teams to tailor their approach based on the unique characteristics of the project. DAD promotes a people-first approach, encouraging collaboration and continuous improvement, which are essential for successful hybrid project management.

Another framework is the Agile-Waterfall Hybrid model, which integrates the iterative nature of agile with the sequential phases of the waterfall methodology. This model is particularly beneficial for projects that have well-defined requirements but also need the flexibility to adapt to changes. In this framework, the initial phases of the project, such as planning and design, follow the waterfall approach, ensuring thorough documentation and stakeholder alignment. Subsequent phases, such as development and testing, adopt agile practices, allowing for iterative progress and regular feedback. This combination ensures that the project benefits from both detailed planning and adaptive execution.

The Scaled Agile Framework (SAFe) is another significant framework that supports hybrid project management. SAFe is designed for large-scale projects that require coordination across multiple teams. It integrates agile principles with lean practices and systems thinking, providing a structured approach to scaling agile practices across an organization. SAFe emphasizes alignment, built-in quality, and transparency, ensuring that all teams work towards common objectives while maintaining the flexibility to respond to changes. This framework is particularly useful for organizations that need to manage complex projects with high interdependencies.

The Project Management Institute's (PMI) Agile Practice Guide also offers valuable insights into hybrid project management. This guide provides practical advice on how to blend agile and traditional practices, focusing on tailoring approaches to fit the specific needs of a project. It highlights the importance of understanding the project environment, stakeholder expectations, and organizational culture when selecting and integrating methodologies. The PMI Agile Practice Guide emphasizes the need for continuous learning and adaptation, encouraging project managers to refine their approach based on ongoing feedback and lessons learned.

In addition to these frameworks, the Hybrid Project Management (HPM) framework offers a tailored approach to integrating agile and traditional methodologies. HPM focuses on identifying the most effective practices from both methodologies and combining them to suit the project's needs. This framework advocates for a flexible approach, allowing project managers to select and adapt practices based on the project's complexity, risk, and stakeholder requirements. HPM emphasizes the importance of communication, collaboration, and adaptability, ensuring that the project team can respond effectively to changes and challenges.

Each of these frameworks offers unique benefits and considerations for integrating hybrid project management approaches. The selection of a framework should be based on the specific needs of the project, the organizational context, and the capabilities of the project team. By leveraging the strengths of both traditional and agile methodologies, hybrid project management frameworks provide a robust foundation for achieving project success in a dynamic and complex environment.

Case Studies of Successful Integration

The hybrid approach to project management has been gaining traction across various industries due to its flexibility and adaptability. This section elucidates the practical application of the hybrid methodology through a series of case studies, demonstrating how organizations have successfully integrated traditional and agile practices to optimize project outcomes.

One notable example is a multinational technology corporation that sought to enhance its product development cycle. Faced with the challenge of maintaining rigorous compliance requirements while accelerating time-to-market, the organization adopted a hybrid framework combining Waterfall and Scrum methodologies. The initial phases of the project, which involved extensive requirements gathering and design, were managed using Waterfall to ensure all regulatory standards were meticulously documented and approved. Subsequently, the development phase transitioned to Scrum, allowing for iterative progress, continuous feedback, and rapid adjustments. This integration resulted in a 30% reduction in development time and a significant improvement in product quality, meeting both regulatory demands and market expectations.

In the healthcare sector, a leading hospital network implemented a hybrid approach to upgrade its electronic health record (EHR) system. The complexity of the project required a structured framework to manage the diverse stakeholder requirements and extensive data migration tasks. The hospital used the Waterfall model for the initial planning and data migration phases to ensure a controlled and predictable process. Concurrently, the agile methodology was employed during the software customization and user training phases. Agile's iterative cycles enabled the project team to incorporate user feedback quickly and adapt the system to the specific needs of healthcare professionals. The hybrid strategy facilitated a seamless transition to the new EHR system, enhancing patient care and operational efficiency.

A financial services company provides another illustrative case. The firm aimed to develop a new mobile banking application to improve customer engagement. Given the high stakes of security and regulatory compliance, the company utilized a hybrid approach by integrating PRINCE2 and Kanban methodologies. The PRINCE2 framework provided a structured governance model to manage risk and compliance aspects, while Kanban facilitated continuous delivery and improvement in the development process. By leveraging the strengths of both methodologies, the company achieved a balanced approach that ensured regulatory compliance and delivered a user-friendly application within the projected timeline and budget.

In the manufacturing industry, a global automotive company faced the challenge of developing a new vehicle model with stringent safety requirements and market-driven timelines. The company employed a hybrid approach by combining Lean Six Sigma and Agile methodologies. Lean Six Sigma was used during the initial design and prototyping phases to eliminate waste and optimize processes. In parallel, Agile was applied in the software development and testing phases to enable rapid iterations and incorporate real-time feedback. This dual approach not only met the safety and quality standards but also accelerated the time-to-market by 20%, providing a competitive edge in the market.

These case studies underscore the versatility and effectiveness of the hybrid approach in diverse sectors. By strategically integrating traditional and agile methodologies, organizations can address specific project challenges, enhance collaboration, and achieve superior results. The successful application of the hybrid model in these cases highlights its potential to transform project management practices, offering a robust framework that adapts to the dynamic needs of modern projects.

Common Pitfalls and How to Avoid Them

In the realm of implementing hybrid project management approaches, numerous challenges and pitfalls can impede the successful execution of projects. A rigorous examination of these common pitfalls, coupled with strategies to mitigate them, is essential for project managers striving to optimize outcomes.

One notable pitfall in hybrid project management is the misalignment between hybrid methodologies and organizational culture. Organizations often possess entrenched practices and cultural norms that may resist change. This misalignment can lead to friction and reduced efficacy of the hybrid approach. To circumvent this issue, it is imperative to conduct a thorough cultural assessment prior to implementation. Engaging stakeholders at all levels and fostering a culture of adaptability can bridge the gap between new methodologies and existing practices.

Another prevalent issue is inadequate training and expertise among team members. Hybrid approaches necessitate a nuanced understanding of both traditional and agile methodologies. Insufficient training can result in improper application of techniques, leading to project delays and inefficiencies. Investing in comprehensive training programs and ongoing professional development ensures that team members are well-versed in the hybrid approach, thereby enhancing their ability to execute projects effectively.

Communication breakdowns pose a significant threat to the success of hybrid projects. The integration of diverse methodologies can create complexities in communication channels and reporting structures. Ambiguities and inconsistencies in communication can lead to misunderstandings and misalignment of project goals. Establishing clear communication protocols and utilizing collaborative tools can streamline information flow and ensure that all stakeholders are aligned.

The complexity of managing resources in a hybrid environment cannot be understated. Resource allocation becomes challenging when balancing the demands of agile and traditional methodologies. Overcommitting resources to one aspect of the project can compromise the other, leading to imbalances and inefficiencies. Implementing robust resource management practices and employing tools that offer visibility into resource allocation can mitigate this risk.

A critical yet often overlooked pitfall is the lack of a well-defined governance framework. Hybrid projects require a governance structure that accommodates the flexibility of agile methods while maintaining the control of traditional approaches. Absence of such a framework can result in governance gaps, leading to project drift and scope creep. Developing a tailored governance model that clearly delineates roles, responsibilities, and decision-making processes is crucial for maintaining project control and direction.

Resistance to change is a ubiquitous challenge in any project management context, and hybrid approaches are no exception. Team members accustomed to traditional methodologies may exhibit reluctance to adopt new practices. This resistance can hinder the seamless integration of hybrid approaches. Addressing this issue involves fostering an environment of openness and inclusivity, where team members feel empowered to contribute to the evolution of project practices.

Lastly, the insufficient integration of tools and technologies can hamper the effectiveness of hybrid project management. The disparate nature of hybrid approaches often necessitates the use of multiple tools, which can lead to fragmentation and inefficiencies. Ensuring the seamless integration of tools and technologies, possibly through the adoption of integrated project management software, can enhance coordination and streamline project workflows.

By identifying and proactively addressing these common pitfalls, project managers can enhance the efficacy of hybrid approaches and drive successful project outcomes. The meticulous application of these strategies not only mitigates risks but also fosters a resilient and adaptable project management environment.

Chapter 5: Planning in a Hybrid Environment

Initial Planning and Scope Definition

The initial phase of applying a hybrid approach to project implementation necessitates meticulous planning and precise scope definition. This phase is critical as it sets the foundation for the project's success, integrating both traditional and agile methodologies to leverage their respective strengths. The objective is to establish a comprehensive framework that guides the project from inception to completion while accommodating flexibility and adaptability.

The first step involves assembling a cross-functional team comprising stakeholders, project managers, and subject matter experts. This team is tasked with identifying the project's objectives, deliverables, and constraints. Engaging stakeholders early in the process ensures that their expectations are aligned with the project goals, thereby minimizing the risk of scope creep and miscommunication.

A detailed project charter is developed to encapsulate the project's vision, mission, and strategic significance. This document serves as a reference point, outlining the project's purpose, key milestones, and success criteria. It is imperative that the charter includes a clear definition of roles and responsibilities, ensuring that each team member understands their contributions and accountability.

Subsequently, a thorough needs assessment is conducted to identify the requirements and expectations of all stakeholders. This assessment involves gathering qualitative and quantitative data through interviews, surveys, and workshops. The data collected is analyzed to prioritize requirements based on their impact on the project's objectives and feasibility. The outcome of this assessment is a well-defined requirements document that serves as the baseline for scope definition.

The scope definition process entails delineating the boundaries of the project, specifying what is included and excluded. This is achieved through the creation of a Work Breakdown Structure (WBS), which decomposes the project into manageable components. Each component is further broken down into tasks and sub-tasks, providing a granular view of the work required. The WBS facilitates the estimation of time, resources, and costs associated with each task, enabling more accurate planning and budgeting.

Risk identification and assessment are integral to the initial planning phase. Potential risks are systematically identified, analyzed, and documented in a risk register. Each risk is evaluated based on its likelihood and impact, and mitigation strategies are devised to address high-priority risks. This proactive approach ensures that the project is better prepared to handle uncertainties, enhancing its resilience.

A hybrid project management plan is then developed, incorporating elements of both traditional and agile methodologies. This plan outlines the project lifecycle, specifying phases, deliverables, and review points. It also includes a communication plan that details how information will be disseminated among stakeholders, ensuring transparency and fostering collaboration.

The project schedule is created using tools such as Gantt charts and Kanban boards, which provide visual representations of the timeline and workflow. These tools facilitate the tracking of progress and identification of potential bottlenecks, enabling timely interventions.

Lastly, a performance measurement baseline is established, encompassing scope, time, and cost baselines. These baselines serve as benchmarks against which the project's performance is measured. Variances from the baselines are monitored through regular status reports and performance reviews, ensuring that corrective actions are taken promptly.

In summary, the initial planning and scope definition phase is a systematic and structured process that lays the groundwork for successful project implementation. By integrating traditional and agile methodologies, this hybrid approach ensures that the project is both well-planned and adaptable to changing circumstances.

Resource Allocation and Management

Effective resource allocation and management are pivotal components in the successful implementation of hybrid project approaches. This subchapter delves into the methodologies and strategies that ensure optimal utilization of resources, balancing the dual demands of agile flexibility and traditional project control.

In hybrid project management, resources encompass human capital, financial assets, technological tools, and time. The complexity arises from the need to harmonize these resources across different project phases, each potentially governed by distinct methodologies. A meticulous planning phase is essential, where resource requirements are identified, quantified, and scheduled. This involves creating a resource breakdown structure (RBS) that aligns with the work breakdown structure (WBS), ensuring that each task has the necessary resources allocated appropriately.

One of the primary challenges in hybrid approaches is the dynamic nature of resource requirements, especially when agile methodologies are integrated. Agile projects often demand rapid reallocation of resources to respond to changing priorities and unforeseen obstacles. Therefore, resource managers must adopt adaptive strategies, utilizing tools such as Kanban boards and resource leveling techniques to maintain a balanced workload. This ensures that resources are neither underutilized nor overburdened, maintaining efficiency and productivity.

Resource allocation in hybrid projects also necessitates a robust communication framework. Regular cross-functional meetings and transparent reporting systems are essential to keep all stakeholders informed about resource status and potential bottlenecks. This transparency facilitates proactive adjustments, mitigating risks associated with resource shortages or surpluses. Additionally, leveraging project management software that integrates resource management features can provide real-time insights and predictive analytics, aiding in more informed decision-making.

Financial resources in hybrid projects require careful budgeting and monitoring. Traditional project management emphasizes detailed upfront budgeting, while agile practices advocate for iterative funding based on incremental progress. A hybrid approach must integrate these philosophies, establishing a flexible yet controlled financial framework. This could involve setting a baseline budget with contingencies for agile iterations, allowing for financial agility without compromising overall fiscal discipline.

Human resource management within hybrid projects poses unique challenges, particularly in terms of skillset alignment and team dynamics. Teams must possess a blend of competencies suitable for both agile and traditional tasks. Continuous training and development programs are crucial to equip team members with the necessary skills and knowledge. Furthermore, fostering a collaborative culture that embraces both agile and traditional mindsets is vital. This can be achieved through team-building activities, shared goals, and a unified project vision.

Technological resources, including software and hardware, must be carefully selected and managed to support hybrid methodologies. Tools that offer flexibility, scalability, and integration capabilities are preferred. For instance, project management platforms that support both agile sprints and Gantt charts can provide a comprehensive view of the project timeline and resource allocation. Regular audits and updates of technological resources ensure they remain aligned with project needs and industry standards.

Time management in hybrid projects requires a dual approach, balancing the rigid timelines of traditional project management with the iterative cycles of agile. Techniques such as timeboxing, where fixed periods are allocated for specific activities, can bridge this gap. Additionally, employing critical path analysis alongside agile burndown charts provides a holistic view of project progress and time allocation.

Strategic resource allocation and management in hybrid projects demand a nuanced understanding of both agile and traditional methodologies. By integrating adaptive planning, robust communication, financial flexibility, skill development, and technological alignment, project managers can navigate the complexities of hybrid resource management, driving successful project outcomes.

Risk Management Strategies

In the realm of project management, particularly within the context of hybrid approaches, effective risk management strategies are paramount to ensuring successful outcomes. Hybrid project management amalgamates elements from both traditional and agile methodologies, thus necessitating a nuanced approach to risk management. The multifaceted nature of hybrid projects introduces a variety of risks that must be meticulously identified, assessed, and mitigated.

One of the foundational strategies in managing risks within hybrid projects involves comprehensive risk identification. This process should be iterative and continuous, leveraging techniques from both agile and traditional frameworks. Traditional risk identification methods, such as SWOT analysis (Strengths, Weaknesses, Opportunities, Threats) and checklists, can be complemented by agile techniques such as daily stand-ups and sprint retrospectives. These agile practices facilitate real-time risk identification, enabling the project team to address issues as they arise.

Quantitative and qualitative risk assessment are integral to understanding the potential impact of identified risks. Quantitative risk analysis employs statistical methods to estimate the probability and impact of risks, often utilizing tools such as Monte Carlo simulations and decision tree analysis. These techniques provide a numerical basis for risk prioritization, which is essential for resource allocation and contingency planning. Conversely, qualitative risk assessment focuses on the subjective evaluation of risks, leveraging expert judgment and risk matrices to categorize and prioritize risks based on their severity and likelihood.

Mitigation strategies must be tailored to the specific nature of hybrid projects, which often combine fixed scope elements with flexible, iterative components. For risks associated with fixed scope elements, traditional mitigation strategies such as thorough planning, robust documentation, and stringent change control processes are effective. These strategies ensure that deviations from the project plan are minimized and controlled.

In contrast, risks inherent to the iterative components of hybrid projects require agile mitigation techniques. These may include adaptive planning, where project plans are continuously refined based on feedback and evolving project conditions. Agile risk mitigation also emphasizes the importance of maintaining a flexible and responsive project environment, enabling the team to pivot and adjust strategies in response to emerging risks. Techniques such as timeboxing and backlog prioritization ensure that the project remains focused on delivering value, even in the face of uncertainty.

Communication plays a critical role in the effective management of risks in hybrid projects. Establishing clear and open channels of communication ensures that all stakeholders are aware of potential risks and their implications. Regular risk review meetings, involving both the project team and key stakeholders, facilitate transparency and collective decision-making. This collaborative approach to risk management fosters a shared understanding of project risks and promotes a proactive stance in addressing them.

Additionally, the integration of risk management tools and software can enhance the efficiency and effectiveness of risk management processes in hybrid projects. These tools enable real-time tracking and analysis of risks, providing the project team with up-to-date information for informed decision-making. Features such as automated risk alerts and dashboards offer a comprehensive overview of the risk landscape, allowing for timely interventions and adjustments.

Incorporating these risk management strategies within hybrid project frameworks not only mitigates potential adverse impacts but also enhances the overall resilience and adaptability of the project. Leveraging a combination of traditional and agile risk management techniques ensures that hybrid projects can navigate the complexities and uncertainties inherent in their execution, ultimately contributing to their successful completion.

Stakeholder Engagement

Effective stakeholder engagement is essential for the successful implementation of a hybrid project management approach. Stakeholders, defined as individuals or groups with an interest or influence in the project, play a critical role in determining its direction and success. Engaging these stakeholders involves identifying their needs and expectations, fostering open communication, and actively involving them in decision-making processes.

Identifying stakeholders is the first step in effective engagement. This involves mapping out all individuals and groups that are affected by or can affect the project. Stakeholders can include project team members, clients, suppliers, regulatory bodies, and the community. Utilizing tools such as stakeholder analysis matrices can help in categorizing stakeholders based on their influence and interest levels. This categorization enables project managers to tailor their engagement strategies accordingly.

Communication is a cornerstone of stakeholder engagement. Clear, consistent, and transparent communication helps build trust and ensures that stakeholders are well-informed about the project's progress and any potential issues. Various communication methods can be employed, including meetings, emails, reports, and dashboards. The choice of communication method should be aligned with the stakeholder's preferences and the nature of the information being conveyed.

Active involvement of stakeholders in the project's decision-making processes enhances their commitment and support. This can be achieved by including stakeholders in key meetings, workshops, and review sessions. Their input can provide valuable insights, foster innovation, and ensure that the project aligns with their expectations. Techniques such as focus groups, surveys, and interviews can be used to gather stakeholder feedback.

Managing stakeholder expectations is crucial to prevent conflicts and ensure project success. This involves setting realistic expectations from the onset and continuously managing them throughout the project lifecycle. Regular updates and transparent communication about project progress, risks, and changes help in managing these expectations. Additionally, addressing any concerns promptly and effectively can prevent misunderstandings and maintain stakeholder support.

Conflict resolution is an integral part of stakeholder engagement. Conflicts may arise due to differing interests, priorities, or perspectives. Effective conflict resolution strategies include active listening, negotiation, and mediation. A structured approach to conflict resolution ensures that disagreements are addressed constructively, preserving stakeholder relationships and maintaining project momentum.

The hybrid project management approach combines elements of traditional and agile methodologies, offering flexibility in stakeholder engagement. Traditional methods, such as detailed planning and documentation, provide a structured framework for stakeholder involvement. Agile methods, with their emphasis on iterative development and continuous feedback, allow for more dynamic and responsive engagement. Balancing these approaches enables project managers to tailor their engagement strategies to the unique needs of the project and its stakeholders.

Measuring the effectiveness of stakeholder engagement is essential for continuous improvement. Key performance indicators (KPIs) such as stakeholder satisfaction, level of engagement, and frequency of communication can be used to assess the success of engagement efforts. Regularly reviewing these metrics and making necessary adjustments ensures that the engagement strategies remain effective and aligned with project goals.

In conclusion, stakeholder engagement is a multifaceted process that requires careful planning, effective communication, active involvement, and continuous improvement. By adopting a hybrid approach, project managers can leverage the strengths of both traditional and agile methodologies to engage stakeholders effectively, ensuring project success.

Chapter 6: Executing Hybrid Projects

Team Collaboration and Communication

Effective team collaboration and communication are pivotal elements in the successful implementation of a hybrid project management approach. The hybrid method integrates the strengths of both Agile and traditional methodologies, necessitating a robust framework for communication and collaboration to ensure cohesion and efficiency.

A hybrid project environment requires clear and consistent communication channels. The complexity of integrating Agile's iterative processes with traditional project's structured phases demands that all team members are well-informed and aligned on project goals, timelines, and deliverables. Regular meetings, such as daily stand-ups or weekly reviews, play a crucial role in maintaining transparency and addressing any issues promptly. These meetings should be structured to provide updates on progress, discuss obstacles, and plan subsequent tasks. Utilizing collaborative tools like Slack, Microsoft Teams, or Trello can enhance real-time communication and document sharing, ensuring that information is accessible to all stakeholders.

The role of the project manager in a hybrid approach is multifaceted. They must possess the ability to navigate both Agile and traditional project management landscapes, facilitating communication between diverse teams. This duality requires a keen understanding of the specific needs and expectations inherent in each methodology. For instance, Agile teams benefit from a more flexible, adaptive communication style, whereas traditional teams may require more formal, scheduled updates. The project manager must bridge these differing communication styles to foster a cohesive team environment.

Collaboration extends beyond mere communication; it encompasses the integration of diverse skill sets and expertise. In a hybrid project, teams often consist of members with varying backgrounds, including developers, designers, analysts, and stakeholders. Encouraging cross-functional collaboration is essential to leverage the full potential of the team's collective knowledge. Techniques such as pair programming, joint application development sessions, and cross-training can enhance collaborative efforts, ensuring that team members are not working in silos but are contributing to a unified project objective.

Stakeholder engagement is a critical aspect of a hybrid approach. Regular updates and feedback loops with stakeholders help align their expectations with the project's progress. This engagement should be structured to provide clear, concise information about the project's status, potential risks, and any necessary adjustments. Utilizing visual aids like Gantt charts, burn-down charts, and Kanban boards can help stakeholders visualize the project's trajectory and understand the interplay between Agile iterations and traditional milestones.

Conflict resolution is another key component of effective team collaboration. The hybrid approach can sometimes lead to misunderstandings or conflicts due to the differing methodologies. Establishing a clear conflict resolution process is essential to address issues swiftly and maintain team morale. This process should encourage open dialogue, active listening, and a focus on finding mutually beneficial solutions. Mediation by the project manager or a designated neutral party can help resolve conflicts and facilitate a harmonious working environment.

Training and continuous improvement are fundamental to maintaining effective collaboration and communication. Providing team members with ongoing training in both Agile and traditional methodologies ensures that they are equipped with the necessary skills to navigate the hybrid approach. Additionally, fostering a culture of continuous improvement through regular retrospectives and feedback sessions can help identify areas for enhancement and implement changes that optimize team performance.

In conclusion, the successful implementation of a hybrid project management approach hinges on effective team collaboration and communication. By establishing clear communication channels, fostering cross-functional collaboration, engaging stakeholders, resolving conflicts, and prioritizing training and continuous improvement, teams can navigate the complexities of a hybrid approach and achieve project success.

Tools and Technologies

The integration of hybrid approaches in project management necessitates a comprehensive understanding of various tools and technologies to ensure successful implementation. These tools and technologies can be broadly categorized into software solutions, collaborative platforms, and methodological frameworks. Each category plays a crucial role in enhancing the efficiency, communication, and overall effectiveness of hybrid project management.

Software solutions form the backbone of hybrid project management, providing functionalities that bridge traditional and agile methodologies. Project management software such as Microsoft Project, Asana, and Jira offer features that support both Waterfall and Agile practices. Microsoft Project excels in detailed planning and resource allocation, making it suitable for the Waterfall approach. On the other hand, Jira is designed with Agile principles in mind, facilitating iterative development and continuous improvement through its robust issue-tracking and sprint planning capabilities. Asana provides a flexible platform that can be tailored to support hybrid models, allowing teams to switch between boards for Agile tasks and timelines for Waterfall planning seamlessly.

Collaborative platforms are essential for maintaining communication and coordination among team members, especially in hybrid environments where teams may be distributed across different locations. Tools like Slack, Microsoft Teams, and Trello enhance real-time communication, file sharing, and task management. Slack integrates with numerous other tools, providing a centralized communication hub that supports both synchronous and asynchronous interactions. Microsoft Teams offers comprehensive collaboration capabilities, including video conferencing, chat, and integration with Office 365 applications. Trello, with its intuitive Kanban boards, allows teams to visualize workflows and manage tasks effectively, supporting both Agile and Waterfall elements within a single project.

Methodological frameworks provide the structural foundation for implementing hybrid approaches. The Scaled Agile Framework (SAFe) and Disciplined Agile Delivery (DAD) are two prominent methodologies that offer guidance on integrating Agile practices at scale within traditional project management environments. SAFe outlines principles and practices for aligning Agile development with organizational objectives, emphasizing collaboration, alignment, and delivery. DAD extends Agile practices by incorporating governance, continuous improvement, and a focus on the entire delivery lifecycle. These frameworks provide a structured approach to blending Agile and traditional methodologies, ensuring that hybrid projects are executed effectively.

The use of cloud-based technologies further enhances the flexibility and scalability of hybrid project management. Cloud platforms such as Amazon Web Services (AWS), Google Cloud Platform (GCP), and Microsoft Azure provide robust infrastructure and services that support dynamic project environments. These platforms offer tools for continuous integration and continuous deployment (CI/CD), enabling teams to automate testing and deployment processes. Additionally, cloud-based storage solutions like Google Drive and Dropbox ensure that project documents and resources are accessible to all team members, regardless of their location.

Data analytics and reporting tools are also critical in hybrid project management, providing insights into project performance and facilitating data-driven decision-making. Tools like Power BI, Tableau, and Google Data Studio enable project managers to create interactive dashboards and visualizations, offering real-time insights into project metrics such as progress, resource utilization, and risk factors. These tools help identify trends, uncover potential issues, and support proactive management strategies.

Incorporating these tools and technologies into hybrid project management practices requires a strategic approach. Project managers must assess the specific needs of their projects, select appropriate tools, and ensure that team members are adequately trained. By leveraging the strengths of both traditional and Agile methodologies, supported by advanced tools and technologies, organizations can achieve greater flexibility, efficiency, and success in their project endeavors.

Monitoring and Controlling

The essence of effectively implementing a hybrid project management approach lies in the meticulous monitoring and controlling of project activities. This subchapter delves into the critical aspects of this phase, elucidating the methods, tools, and best practices necessary to ensure project objectives are met within the constraints of scope, time, cost, and quality.

The hybrid approach, which amalgamates traditional (waterfall) and agile methodologies, necessitates a versatile and adaptive monitoring and controlling framework. This framework must cater to the linear progression of certain project elements while accommodating the iterative and incremental nature of others. Key performance indicators (KPIs) and metrics are indispensable in this context. They provide quantifiable measures to assess progress and performance. Common KPIs include schedule variance, cost variance, earned value metrics, and defect density. These indicators must be carefully selected to reflect both the predictive and adaptive components of the hybrid model.

A critical component of monitoring in hybrid projects is the integration of project management software tools. These tools facilitate real-time data collection, analysis, and reporting, enabling project managers to maintain an up-to-date view of project status. Tools such as Microsoft Project, JIRA, and Trello are frequently employed, each offering functionalities that cater to both waterfall and agile methodologies. For instance, Gantt charts in Microsoft Project can be used to track linear tasks, whereas JIRA's Kanban boards are effective in managing iterative work cycles.

Risk management is another pivotal element in the monitoring and controlling phase. Hybrid projects, by their very nature, are susceptible to a diverse range of risks. These include risks associated with scope creep in agile components and risks related to rigid timelines in waterfall components. A robust risk management plan should be in place, encompassing risk identification, analysis, response planning, and monitoring. Regular risk audits and reviews are essential to ensure that potential threats are identified and mitigated promptly.

Stakeholder communication is vital during the monitoring and controlling phase. Transparent and frequent communication ensures that stakeholders are kept informed of project progress, issues, and changes. This can be achieved through regular status meetings, progress reports, and dashboards. Agile ceremonies such as daily stand-ups, sprint reviews, and retrospectives should be integrated with traditional status reporting mechanisms to provide a comprehensive view of project health.

Change control processes must be meticulously managed to balance the flexibility of agile with the stability of waterfall. An effective change control board (CCB) should be established to evaluate and approve changes. This board should include representatives from both the agile and waterfall teams to ensure that changes are assessed from multiple perspectives.

Change requests should be documented, analyzed for impact, and communicated to all relevant stakeholders.

Quality assurance and control are integral to maintaining the standards of deliverables. In a hybrid project, quality control activities must be tailored to suit both agile and waterfall components. Agile techniques such as continuous integration and automated testing can be employed alongside traditional quality control measures like inspections and reviews. This dual approach ensures that quality is built into the product from the outset and maintained throughout the project lifecycle.

In conclusion, the monitoring and controlling phase of a hybrid project management approach is multifaceted, requiring a blend of traditional and agile techniques. By leveraging appropriate tools, maintaining rigorous risk management, ensuring transparent stakeholder communication, implementing robust change control processes, and adhering to stringent quality assurance measures, project managers can effectively navigate the complexities of hybrid projects and steer them towards successful completion.

Quality Assurance

Quality assurance (QA) within the realm of hybrid project management is a multifaceted discipline that ensures the deliverables meet the predefined standards and specifications. The hybrid approach, which amalgamates traditional and agile methodologies, necessitates a comprehensive and adaptive QA strategy to accommodate the dynamic nature of project execution.

The core objective of QA in a hybrid project is to maintain a balance between flexibility and control. This involves integrating QA practices that are consistent with both agile and traditional methods. Agile practices emphasize continuous testing and iterative feedback, while traditional methodologies often focus on extensive upfront planning and phase-gate reviews. A hybrid QA framework leverages the strengths of both approaches to mitigate risks and enhance the quality of project outcomes.

In the planning phase, the QA strategy must be clearly defined. This includes setting quality objectives, identifying key performance indicators (KPIs), and developing a detailed QA plan. The QA plan should outline the standards, procedures, and tools that will be employed throughout the project lifecycle. Risk assessment and management are integral components at this stage, identifying potential quality issues and devising mitigation strategies.

During the execution phase, QA activities must be seamlessly integrated into the project workflow. This involves continuous monitoring and control processes to ensure adherence to quality standards. Agile practices, such as daily stand-ups, sprint reviews, and retrospectives, play a crucial role in maintaining quality. These practices facilitate early detection and resolution of defects, ensuring that quality is built into the product incrementally.

Traditional QA practices, such as formal inspections, audits, and testing phases, are also essential. These practices provide a structured approach to validating that the project deliverables meet the required standards. Inspections and audits help in identifying deviations from the quality plan and implementing corrective actions. Testing phases, including unit testing, integration testing, system testing, and user acceptance testing (UAT), ensure that the final product is free of defects and meets the user requirements.

Hybrid projects often involve diverse teams and stakeholders, making communication and collaboration critical to QA success. Effective communication channels must be established to ensure that all team members are aware of the quality requirements and their roles in achieving them. Collaborative tools and platforms can facilitate real-time information sharing and feedback, enhancing the overall QA process.

Automation plays a significant role in hybrid QA. Automated testing tools can streamline repetitive testing tasks, increase test coverage, and reduce human error. Continuous integration and continuous deployment (CI/CD) pipelines can be leveraged to automate the build, test, and deployment processes, ensuring that quality checks are performed consistently and efficiently.

QA metrics and reporting are vital for tracking progress and making informed decisions. Key metrics, such as defect density, test coverage, and mean time to resolution (MTTR), provide insights into the quality of the project deliverables. Regular reporting and dashboards help project managers and stakeholders to monitor quality performance and take timely corrective actions.

A robust QA framework in a hybrid project not only ensures the delivery of high-quality products but also fosters a culture of continuous improvement. By integrating agile and traditional QA practices, hybrid projects can achieve a balance between adaptability and rigor, ultimately leading to successful project outcomes.

Chapter 7: Leadership in Hybrid Project Management

Leadership Styles and Their Impact

The implementation of a hybrid approach in project management necessitates an understanding of various leadership styles and their respective impacts on project outcomes. Leadership styles are pivotal in shaping the dynamics of a project team, influencing both the processes and the results. The following discussion delineates various leadership styles and their effects on the implementation of hybrid project management methodologies.

Transformational leadership, characterized by the ability to inspire and motivate team members towards achieving a collective vision, is particularly effective in hybrid project environments. This style fosters innovation and adaptability, essential traits for managing the complexity and fluidity inherent in hybrid projects. Transformational leaders encourage team members to transcend their self-interests for the sake of the project, thereby enhancing team cohesion and commitment. The resultant high levels of motivation and engagement can lead to superior project performance and successful implementation of hybrid methodologies.

Conversely, transactional leadership, which emphasizes structured tasks, clear goals, and rewards or penalties based on performance, may have limited applicability in hybrid project settings. While this style ensures discipline and adherence to established protocols, it may stifle creativity and flexibility, critical components in hybrid approaches. The rigidity of transactional leadership could potentially hinder the dynamic and iterative processes that hybrid methodologies often entail. However, in phases of the project requiring strict adherence to timelines and deliverables, transactional leadership can provide the necessary structure and accountability.

Servant leadership, focusing on the growth and well-being of team members, can significantly impact the implementation of hybrid project management. By prioritizing the needs of the team, servant leaders create a supportive environment that nurtures collaboration and trust. This approach aligns well with the hybrid model's emphasis on teamwork and collective problem-solving. Servant leadership can lead to higher levels of team satisfaction and retention, which are crucial for maintaining continuity and momentum in hybrid projects.

Situational leadership, which advocates for the adaptation of leadership style based on the maturity and competence of team members, is particularly relevant for hybrid project management. This flexibility allows leaders to provide the appropriate level of guidance and support as the project evolves. For instance, during the initial stages of a project, a more directive approach may be necessary to establish clear objectives and processes. As the project progresses and the team gains confidence and competence, a more delegative style can empower team members to take ownership and drive innovation. The adaptability inherent in situational leadership can enhance the effectiveness of hybrid methodologies by ensuring that leadership interventions are contextually appropriate.

Autocratic leadership, characterized by centralization of decision-making and unilateral control, may be less effective in hybrid project environments that thrive on collaboration and flexibility. While this style can be beneficial in crisis situations requiring swift decision-making, its overuse can lead to disengagement and reduced morale among team members. The hybrid approach's reliance on iterative feedback and collective input may be undermined by autocratic tendencies, potentially compromising the project's adaptive capacity.

Democratic leadership, which emphasizes participative decision-making and shared responsibility, aligns well with the collaborative nature of hybrid project management. By involving team members in the decision-making process, democratic leaders can harness diverse perspectives and foster a sense of ownership and accountability. This inclusive approach can enhance problem-solving capabilities and drive innovative solutions, critical for the successful implementation of hybrid methodologies.

Understanding the nuanced impacts of different leadership styles is crucial for effectively implementing hybrid project management. Leaders must judiciously apply various styles to navigate the complexities and demands of hybrid projects, ensuring that their approach fosters innovation, collaboration, and adaptability.

Building High-Performing Teams

High-performing teams are pivotal to the successful implementation of hybrid project management approaches. These teams are characterized by a synergetic blend of skills, a shared vision, and a commitment to achieving project goals efficiently and effectively. The foundation of a high-performing team lies in the careful selection of team members, fostering a collaborative culture, and implementing robust communication strategies.

The selection of team members is a critical initial step. It involves identifying individuals who not only possess the necessary technical skills but also exhibit strong interpersonal abilities. A hybrid project environment demands flexibility and adaptability, thus team members should be adept at navigating both agile and traditional project management methodologies. This dual competence ensures that the team can seamlessly transition between different phases of the project, leveraging the strengths of each approach.

Creating a collaborative culture is essential for the cohesion and productivity of the team. Leadership plays a crucial role in this aspect. Leaders must encourage open communication, mutual respect, and trust among team members. Regular team-building activities and workshops can help in breaking down barriers and fostering a sense of unity. Moreover, recognizing and rewarding collective achievements can motivate team members to strive for excellence.

Communication is the lifeblood of any high-performing team. In a hybrid project setup, clear and consistent communication is paramount to ensure that all team members are aligned with the project objectives and timelines. Utilizing a combination of synchronous and asynchronous communication tools can enhance information flow. Regular meetings, such as daily stand-ups and weekly reviews, provide platforms for discussing progress, addressing challenges, and realigning efforts. Additionally, collaborative tools like project management software can facilitate real-time updates and documentation, ensuring transparency and accountability.

Effective conflict resolution mechanisms are also vital. Conflicts, if not managed properly, can derail the project. Establishing clear protocols for conflict resolution, including mediation and negotiation techniques, helps in maintaining harmony within the team. Leaders should be trained to identify early signs of conflict and intervene promptly to mitigate any negative impact.

Furthermore, continuous learning and improvement should be ingrained in the team's ethos. Encouraging team members to pursue professional development opportunities, such as certifications and workshops, keeps their skills relevant and sharp. Conducting regular retrospectives allows the team to reflect on their performance, identify areas for improvement, and implement corrective actions.

The integration of diverse perspectives and expertise enhances the problem-solving capabilities of the team. Diversity in terms of gender, ethnicity, and professional background brings in a wealth of ideas and approaches, fostering innovation. Inclusive practices should be adopted to ensure that all voices are heard and valued.

Incorporating feedback mechanisms is another crucial aspect. Soliciting feedback from team members, stakeholders, and clients provides valuable insights into the team's performance and areas needing improvement. Constructive feedback loops help in refining processes and enhancing the overall efficiency of the team.

In conclusion, building high-performing teams in a hybrid project management environment requires a strategic approach encompassing careful selection of team members, fostering a collaborative culture, ensuring robust communication, managing conflicts effectively, promoting continuous learning, embracing diversity, and incorporating feedback mechanisms. These elements collectively contribute to the creation of teams that are not only efficient and productive but also resilient and adaptive to the dynamic demands of hybrid project management.

Conflict Resolution

Effective conflict resolution is paramount in the successful implementation of hybrid project management approaches, which combine elements of traditional and agile methodologies. This chapter delves into the strategies and practices essential for resolving conflicts that may arise due to the inherent differences in these methodologies.

A crucial first step in conflict resolution is the identification and acknowledgment of the sources of conflict. In hybrid project environments, conflicts often stem from discrepancies in expectations, communication styles, and decision-making processes. Traditional project management typically emphasizes a structured, hierarchical approach, while agile methodologies prioritize flexibility, collaboration, and iterative progress. These fundamental differences can lead to misunderstandings and disagreements among team members and stakeholders.

To address these conflicts, it is essential to establish a clear conflict resolution framework that incorporates both traditional and agile principles. This framework should include well-defined roles and responsibilities, transparent communication channels, and a systematic approach to conflict identification and resolution. Regular training and workshops can help team members understand the hybrid approach better and foster a culture of mutual respect and collaboration.

Open and effective communication is a cornerstone of conflict resolution in hybrid project management. Encouraging team members to voice their concerns and opinions in a constructive manner can prevent conflicts from escalating. Utilizing tools such as regular stand-up meetings, retrospectives, and feedback sessions can facilitate open dialogue and ensure that issues are addressed promptly. Additionally, employing conflict resolution techniques such as active listening, empathy, and negotiation can help to bridge the gap between differing viewpoints.

Another critical aspect of conflict resolution is the role of the project manager. The project manager must act as a mediator, balancing the needs and expectations of both traditional and agile team members. This requires a deep understanding of both methodologies and the ability to adapt conflict resolution strategies accordingly. The project manager should also be adept at identifying potential conflicts early and intervening before they escalate.

Leveraging collaborative tools and technologies can also aid in conflict resolution. Project management software that integrates features from both traditional and agile methodologies can provide a unified platform for tracking progress, managing tasks, and facilitating communication. These tools can help to minimize misunderstandings and provide a clear overview of the project status, which is crucial for resolving conflicts.

It is also important to establish a culture of continuous improvement and learning within the team. Encouraging team members to reflect on past conflicts and their resolutions can provide valuable insights and improve future conflict resolution processes. Implementing regular review and feedback mechanisms can help to identify areas for improvement and ensure that the team is continuously evolving and adapting to the hybrid approach.

Incorporating conflict resolution best practices from both traditional and agile methodologies can create a more cohesive and collaborative project environment. For instance, traditional methodologies emphasize structured problem-solving techniques, while agile methodologies focus on iterative feedback and adaptation. Combining these approaches can lead to a more comprehensive conflict resolution strategy that addresses the unique challenges of hybrid project management.

Ultimately, effective conflict resolution in hybrid project management requires a proactive and adaptive approach. By understanding the sources of conflict, fostering open communication, leveraging collaborative tools, and promoting a culture of continuous improvement, project teams can navigate the complexities of hybrid methodologies and achieve successful project outcomes.

Motivating Team Members

Motivating team members is a critical component in the successful implementation of a hybrid project management approach. This subchapter examines the essential strategies and theoretical frameworks that can be leveraged to foster motivation within project teams, thereby enhancing productivity and ensuring project success.

Effective motivation begins with understanding the diverse needs and intrinsic drivers of team members. According to Maslow's hierarchy of needs, individuals are motivated by a progression of needs ranging from physiological necessities to self-actualization. In the context of project management, addressing these needs can be operationalized by ensuring a safe and comfortable work environment, providing opportunities for professional growth, and recognizing individual achievements to foster a sense of belonging and self-worth.

Herzberg's two-factor theory further delineates motivation into hygiene factors and motivators. Hygiene factors, such as salary, work conditions, and company policies, must be adequately addressed to prevent dissatisfaction. However, true motivation stems from intrinsic factors like recognition, responsibility, and opportunities for advancement. In hybrid project management, it is imperative to create an environment where these intrinsic motivators are prevalent. For instance, assigning meaningful tasks that align with individual skills and career goals can significantly enhance motivation.

Self-Determination Theory (SDT) posits that motivation is driven by the need for autonomy, competence, and relatedness. Facilitating an autonomous work environment where team members have the freedom to make decisions can lead to higher engagement and creativity. Competence can be fostered through continuous learning opportunities and constructive feedback, enabling team members to feel capable and effective in their roles. Relatedness can be enhanced by promoting a collaborative culture where team members feel connected and valued.

The hybrid approach to project management, which combines elements of both traditional and agile methodologies, provides unique opportunities to implement these motivational strategies. Agile practices, such as daily stand-ups, sprint reviews, and retrospectives, inherently support frequent feedback and recognition, thereby satisfying the need for competence and relatedness. Traditional project management techniques, such as detailed planning and clear role definitions, can help in addressing hygiene factors and providing a structured environment that supports autonomy.

Leadership style plays a pivotal role in motivation. Transformational leadership, characterized by the ability to inspire and intellectually stimulate team members, has been shown to positively impact motivation. Leaders in a hybrid project environment should focus on articulating a compelling vision, providing individualized consideration, and encouraging innovative thinking. This can be achieved through regular one-on-one meetings, personalized development plans, and fostering an open culture where new ideas are welcomed and evaluated.

Moreover, goal-setting theory emphasizes the importance of setting clear, challenging, and attainable goals. In the hybrid project setting, goals should be aligned with both the overall project objectives and individual aspirations. Utilizing SMART (Specific, Measurable, Achievable, Relevant, Time-bound) criteria can ensure that goals are well-defined and motivating. Regularly reviewing and adjusting these goals based on feedback and project progress can maintain motivation and drive continuous improvement.

The role of recognition cannot be understated. Implementing a structured recognition program that celebrates both individual and team achievements can significantly boost morale and motivation. This can include formal awards, public acknowledgments during meetings, and informal gestures such as thank-you notes or team outings. Recognition should be timely, specific, and aligned with the values and goals of the project to be most effective.

In conclusion, motivating team members in a hybrid project management environment requires a multifaceted approach that integrates psychological theories, leadership practices, and structured recognition programs. By understanding and addressing the intrinsic and extrinsic factors that drive motivation, project managers can create a conducive environment that not only enhances individual satisfaction but also drives project success.

Chapter 8: Communication Strategies

Effective Communication Channels

Effective communication channels are fundamental in the successful implementation of a hybrid project management approach. The hybrid model integrates traditional and agile methodologies, necessitating a versatile and multifaceted communication strategy. This subchapter examines the various communication channels that can be employed to enhance collaboration, ensure transparency, and facilitate efficient information flow within hybrid project environments.

In hybrid project management, the selection of appropriate communication channels is crucial. The choice of channels should align with the project's complexity, stakeholder preferences, and the nature of the information being conveyed. Commonly used channels include face-to-face meetings, emails, instant messaging platforms, video conferencing, and project management software.

Face-to-face meetings remain a cornerstone of effective communication, particularly for activities requiring high levels of interaction and problem-solving. These meetings facilitate immediate feedback, foster team cohesion, and allow for the nuanced interpretation of non-verbal cues. However, the hybrid model often involves distributed teams, making it necessary to complement in-person meetings with virtual communication tools.

Emails provide a formal and documented means of communication, suitable for conveying detailed information, sharing important updates, and maintaining a record of correspondence. Despite their advantages, emails can be less effective for prompt discussions and may lead to information overload if not managed properly. To mitigate these issues, project managers should establish clear guidelines on email usage, such as specifying appropriate subjects, concise content, and timely responses.

Instant messaging platforms, such as Slack or Microsoft Teams, offer real-time communication capabilities, fostering quick exchanges and collaborative problem-solving. These platforms are particularly useful for agile components of hybrid projects, where rapid decision-making and iterative feedback are essential. However, the informal nature of instant messaging can sometimes lead to misunderstandings or misinterpretations. Establishing norms for professional conduct and clarity in messaging can help address these challenges.

Video conferencing tools, including Zoom and Google Meet, bridge the gap between face-to-face meetings and virtual communication. They enable visual and auditory interaction, making them suitable for team meetings, stakeholder presentations, and remote collaboration sessions. Effective use of video conferencing requires attention to technical aspects, such as stable internet connections and high-quality audio-visual equipment, as well as soft skills like active listening and clear articulation.

Project management software, such as Jira, Trello, or Asana, integrates communication with task tracking and progress monitoring. These platforms provide a centralized repository for project-related information, facilitating transparency and accountability. They support various communication features, including comment threads, file sharing, and notifications, allowing team members to stay informed and engaged. The use of such tools can significantly enhance coordination and streamline workflows in hybrid projects.

The effectiveness of communication channels in hybrid project management is also influenced by the organizational culture and the team's communication skills. Encouraging an open and inclusive communication environment, where team members feel comfortable sharing ideas and feedback, is essential. Training programs aimed at improving communication skills, such as active listening, conflict resolution, and effective presentation, can further enhance the team's ability to collaborate effectively.

Incorporating a diverse array of communication channels is vital for the dynamic and flexible nature of hybrid project management. By carefully selecting and optimizing these channels, project managers can ensure that information flows seamlessly, stakeholders remain informed and engaged, and the project progresses smoothly towards its objectives. The strategic use of communication channels, tailored to the unique demands of hybrid projects, ultimately contributes to their successful implementation.

Stakeholder Communication

Effective communication with stakeholders is crucial in the implementation of a hybrid project management approach. The integration of traditional and agile methodologies necessitates a nuanced understanding of stakeholder expectations and the ability to convey information transparently and effectively. This subchapter explores the strategies and methodologies required to maintain robust stakeholder communication throughout the lifecycle of hybrid projects.

Stakeholders in hybrid projects often encompass a diverse range of individuals and groups, including project sponsors, team members, customers, and external partners. Each of these stakeholders brings unique perspectives, expectations, and requirements to the project. Therefore, establishing a clear communication plan is essential. This plan should outline the frequency, channels, and type of information to be shared with each stakeholder group. Effective communication plans are adaptive and consider the dynamic nature of stakeholder needs and project progress.

One of the key challenges in stakeholder communication within hybrid projects is the alignment of expectations. Traditional project management approaches emphasize detailed upfront planning and documentation, whereas agile methodologies prioritize iterative development and flexibility. Bridging these differing expectations requires a tailored communication strategy that highlights the benefits and trade-offs of the hybrid approach. Regular updates and transparent reporting mechanisms can help manage expectations and ensure that all stakeholders are informed about the project's status and any changes that may arise.

The use of collaborative tools and platforms is instrumental in facilitating effective stakeholder communication. These tools enable real-time information sharing, feedback collection, and collaborative decision-making. For instance, project management software that integrates both traditional and agile features can provide a centralized repository for project documentation, progress tracking, and stakeholder communication. Such tools enhance transparency and ensure that all stakeholders have access to the information they need to make informed decisions.

Meetings and workshops play a critical role in stakeholder communication. Regularly scheduled meetings, such as sprint reviews, project status updates, and stakeholder briefings, provide opportunities for direct interaction and feedback. These meetings should be structured to address the specific needs of different stakeholder groups and should encourage active participation and dialogue. Workshops, on the other hand, can be used to facilitate collaborative problem-solving and decision-making, particularly when complex issues arise that require input from multiple stakeholders.

Another important aspect of stakeholder communication is the management of stakeholder feedback. Feedback from stakeholders should be actively solicited, systematically documented, and thoughtfully addressed. This feedback loop not only helps in identifying potential issues early but also fosters a sense of ownership and engagement among stakeholders. It is important to establish clear mechanisms for capturing and responding to feedback, ensuring that stakeholders feel heard and valued.

Cultural and organizational factors also influence stakeholder communication in hybrid projects. Understanding the organizational culture and the communication preferences of different stakeholder groups can help tailor communication strategies to be more effective. For example, some stakeholders may prefer formal, written communication, while others may favor informal, verbal updates. Being cognizant of these preferences and adapting communication styles accordingly can enhance the effectiveness of stakeholder interactions.

In conclusion, maintaining effective communication with stakeholders in hybrid projects requires a strategic approach that considers the diverse needs and expectations of different stakeholder groups. By leveraging collaborative tools, regular meetings, and feedback mechanisms, project managers can ensure that stakeholders are well-informed, engaged, and aligned with the project's objectives. Understanding and adapting to cultural and organizational factors further enhances the effectiveness of stakeholder communication, ultimately contributing to the successful implementation of hybrid project management approaches.

Feedback Mechanisms

Feedback mechanisms are integral to the successful implementation of a hybrid project management approach. These mechanisms serve as the backbone for continuous improvement, enabling teams to adapt and refine their processes in real-time. The dynamic nature of hybrid projects, which often combine elements from both Agile and traditional methodologies, requires a robust feedback system to ensure alignment with project goals and stakeholder expectations.

One of the primary feedback mechanisms in a hybrid approach is the iterative review cycle. This cycle typically involves scheduled review meetings at the end of each iteration or phase. During these meetings, team members assess progress, identify any deviations from the project plan, and discuss potential improvements. This iterative process allows for the early detection of issues, reducing the risk of project delays and cost overruns. Moreover, it fosters a culture of transparency and accountability, as team members are encouraged to openly share their insights and concerns.

Another critical feedback mechanism is stakeholder engagement. Regular communication with stakeholders is essential to gather feedback on project deliverables and ensure that their needs are being met. This can be achieved through various channels, such as status updates, demonstration sessions, and feedback surveys. By actively involving stakeholders in the feedback process, project managers can gain valuable insights that can be used to refine project requirements and adjust the project plan as needed. This proactive approach helps to build trust and ensures that the project remains aligned with stakeholder expectations.

Performance metrics also play a crucial role in feedback mechanisms. These metrics, which can include key performance indicators (KPIs), velocity charts, and burn-down charts, provide quantitative data on project performance. By regularly monitoring these metrics, project managers can identify trends and patterns that may indicate potential issues. For example, a declining velocity chart may suggest that the team is struggling to meet its commitments, prompting a review of resource allocation and team capacity. Similarly, an upward trend in defect rates might indicate a need for additional quality assurance measures. By leveraging performance metrics, project managers can make data-driven decisions to optimize project performance.

Retrospectives are another valuable feedback mechanism in hybrid project management. These sessions, typically held at the end of each iteration or phase, provide an opportunity for the team to reflect on what went well, what did not, and what can be improved. Retrospectives encourage a culture of continuous learning and improvement, as team members are encouraged to share their experiences and suggest actionable changes. The insights gained from retrospectives can be used to refine processes, enhance team collaboration, and improve overall project outcomes.

Incorporating feedback loops into the project management process is essential for maintaining agility and responsiveness. Hybrid projects often require a flexible approach to accommodate changing requirements and evolving project landscapes. Feedback mechanisms enable teams to quickly adapt to these changes, ensuring that the project remains on track and delivers value to stakeholders.

Effective communication is the cornerstone of successful feedback mechanisms. Clear and open communication channels facilitate the timely exchange of information, enabling teams to respond swiftly to feedback and make informed decisions. This includes not only formal communication methods, such as meetings and reports, but also informal interactions, such as daily stand-ups and peer reviews. By fostering a culture of open communication, project managers can ensure that feedback is effectively captured and acted upon.

In summary, feedback mechanisms are a vital component of hybrid project management. They enable continuous improvement, foster stakeholder engagement, provide valuable performance data, and promote a culture of learning and adaptation. By effectively implementing these mechanisms, project managers can enhance project outcomes and ensure the successful delivery of hybrid projects.

Managing Remote Teams

The effective management of remote teams has become increasingly vital in the context of hybrid project implementation. This subchapter delves into the principles, challenges, and strategies pertinent to overseeing geographically dispersed teams, ensuring that projects are executed efficiently and cohesively.

Effective communication stands as the cornerstone of remote team management. The absence of physical proximity necessitates the utilization of advanced communication tools to bridge the gap between team members. Synchronous communication platforms like Zoom and Microsoft Teams enable real-time discussions, while asynchronous tools such as Slack and email facilitate ongoing dialogue and information sharing. Establishing clear communication protocols is essential to mitigate misunderstandings and ensure that all team members are aligned with project objectives. Regular virtual meetings, coupled with periodic check-ins, foster a sense of unity and keep the team on track.

Trust and accountability are pivotal in remote team dynamics. The lack of face-to-face interaction can sometimes lead to a diminished sense of responsibility among team members. Implementing a robust accountability framework, which includes setting clear expectations, defining roles, and establishing measurable goals, is crucial. Utilizing project management software such as Trello, Asana, or Jira can aid in tracking progress and ensuring transparency. Regular performance reviews and feedback sessions further reinforce accountability and provide opportunities for continuous improvement.

Remote teams often face the challenge of maintaining team cohesion and morale. The physical separation can lead to feelings of isolation and detachment among team members. Promoting a strong team culture through virtual team-building activities and social events can mitigate these issues. Encouraging informal interactions, such as virtual coffee breaks or online gaming sessions, helps build rapport and fosters a sense of belonging. Additionally, recognizing and celebrating achievements, both big and small, can boost morale and motivate team members.

Time zone differences present another significant challenge in managing remote teams. Coordinating tasks and meetings across different time zones requires careful planning and flexibility.

Utilizing time zone management tools and adopting a flexible working schedule can help accommodate the diverse availability of team members. Establishing a core overlap period, where all team members are available for synchronous communication, can facilitate collaboration and ensure that critical issues are addressed promptly.

The integration of technology plays a crucial role in remote team management. Leveraging cloud-based collaboration tools, such as Google Workspace or Microsoft 365, enables seamless document sharing and real-time collaboration. These tools facilitate version control, ensuring that all team members have access to the latest project documents and resources. Additionally, employing virtual private networks (VPNs) and implementing robust cybersecurity measures are essential to protect sensitive project data and maintain confidentiality.

Effective leadership is paramount in managing remote teams. Leaders must exhibit strong communication skills, empathy, and adaptability to navigate the complexities of remote work. Providing clear direction, offering support, and fostering an inclusive environment are key leadership attributes. Encouraging autonomy and empowering team members to take ownership of their tasks can enhance productivity and innovation. Moreover, leaders should remain vigilant to the well-being of their team members, offering support and resources to address any challenges they may face.

In the realm of hybrid project implementation, the successful management of remote teams hinges on a multifaceted approach that encompasses effective communication, trust and accountability, team cohesion, time zone management, technological integration, and strong leadership. By addressing these elements, project managers can harness the full potential of their remote teams, driving project success and fostering a collaborative and productive work environment.

Chapter 9: Risk Management in Hybrid Projects

Identifying Risks

The identification of risks in a hybrid project management environment necessitates a comprehensive and systematic approach to ensure the successful implementation of projects. A hybrid approach, which integrates elements from various project management methodologies such as Agile, Waterfall, and Lean, introduces unique challenges and opportunities for risk identification. The diverse nature of hybrid projects, combining iterative development with structured phases, requires a nuanced understanding of potential risk factors.

The first step in identifying risks involves establishing a clear and detailed project scope. A well-defined scope serves as the foundation for recognizing areas where uncertainties and potential issues may arise. This includes delineating project objectives, deliverables, timelines, and resource allocations. Precise scope definition helps in pinpointing specific aspects of the project that are susceptible to risks, enabling the project team to focus their risk identification efforts effectively.

Engaging stakeholders early in the project lifecycle is crucial for comprehensive risk identification. Stakeholders, including project sponsors, team members, clients, and end-users, provide valuable insights into potential risks based on their diverse perspectives and experiences. Conducting stakeholder interviews, workshops, and brainstorming sessions facilitates the collection of varied viewpoints, enhancing the identification of risks that may not be immediately apparent to the project team.

Utilizing a risk breakdown structure (RBS) is an effective technique for categorizing and organizing potential risks. An RBS is a hierarchical representation of risks, arranged by categories such as technical, organizational, external, and project management risks. This structured approach aids in systematically identifying risks across different dimensions of the project, ensuring a comprehensive assessment. For hybrid projects, the RBS should be tailored to reflect the integration of multiple methodologies, capturing risks specific to each method as well as those arising from their interaction.

Historical data and lessons learned from previous projects are invaluable resources for identifying risks. Analyzing past projects with similar characteristics can reveal common risk factors and provide insights into effective mitigation strategies. Project teams should maintain a repository of historical data, including risk registers, post-mortem reports, and performance metrics, to facilitate the identification of recurring risks and inform proactive risk management.

The complexity of hybrid projects necessitates the use of advanced risk identification tools and techniques. Techniques such as SWOT analysis (Strengths, Weaknesses, Opportunities, Threats), failure mode and effects analysis (FMEA), and root cause analysis (RCA) provide structured approaches to uncovering potential risks. These techniques enable the project team to systematically evaluate different aspects of the project, identify vulnerabilities, and assess the potential impact of identified risks.

Regular and iterative risk identification is essential in hybrid project management. The dynamic nature of hybrid projects, characterized by ongoing iterations and phased development, requires continuous monitoring and reassessment of risks. Establishing a risk identification schedule, aligned with project milestones and iterations, ensures that new risks are identified promptly and existing risks are re-evaluated in the context of project progress.

Effective communication and documentation are critical components of the risk identification process. Clear and concise documentation of identified risks, along with their potential impact and likelihood, provides a reference for ongoing risk management activities. Utilizing collaborative tools and platforms facilitates real-time communication and updates, ensuring that all project stakeholders are informed of current risks and their status.

In conclusion, the identification of risks in hybrid project management requires a methodical and multi-faceted approach. By leveraging detailed project scope, stakeholder engagement, structured categorization, historical data, advanced techniques, iterative processes, and effective communication, project teams can comprehensively identify risks and lay the foundation for successful risk management.

Risk Assessment Techniques

Risk assessment is a critical component in the implementation of hybrid approaches to project management. It serves as the foundation for identifying, analyzing, and prioritizing potential risks that could impact the project's success. Various risk assessment techniques are available, each with its unique advantages and applications. This subchapter explores several prominent methodologies, emphasizing their relevance and utility in the context of hybrid project management.

One of the most widely recognized techniques is the SWOT analysis, which stands for Strengths, Weaknesses, Opportunities, and Threats. This method provides a comprehensive overview by examining both internal and external factors that could influence the project. Strengths and weaknesses are internal factors that can be controlled or managed, while opportunities and threats are external factors that require strategic planning to mitigate. By systematically addressing each quadrant, project managers can develop a balanced view of potential risks and opportunities, allowing for more informed decision-making.

Another essential technique is the Failure Mode and Effects Analysis (FMEA). This method focuses on identifying potential failure modes within a system or process and evaluating their effects on project outcomes. FMEA involves a detailed examination of each component, assessing the severity, occurrence, and detection of potential failures. The results are typically quantified using a Risk Priority Number (RPN), which helps prioritize risks based on their potential impact. FMEA is particularly useful in complex projects where interdependencies and technical intricacies can lead to unforeseen issues.

The Monte Carlo simulation offers a quantitative approach to risk assessment by using statistical methods to model the probability of different outcomes. This technique involves running numerous simulations with varying input parameters to generate a range of possible scenarios. The results provide a probabilistic distribution of potential project outcomes, enabling managers to understand the likelihood of different risks materializing. Monte Carlo simulations are invaluable for projects with inherent uncertainties and those requiring precise risk quantification.

The Delphi method is another valuable tool, especially for projects requiring expert judgment. This technique involves a structured process where a panel of experts provides independent assessments of potential risks. The responses are then aggregated and analyzed to identify consensus or divergence in opinions. The iterative nature of the Delphi method allows for refinement and validation of risk assessments, making it particularly effective for complex or novel projects where empirical data may be limited.

Risk matrices are also commonly used due to their simplicity and visual appeal. These matrices plot the likelihood of risks against their potential impact, creating a visual representation that helps prioritize risks. By categorizing risks into different zones (e.g., high, medium, low), project managers can quickly identify which risks require immediate attention and which can be monitored over time. This technique is often used in conjunction with other methods to provide a more holistic view of the risk landscape.

Scenario planning involves developing detailed narratives about different future states of the project environment. These scenarios consider various external factors such as market trends, regulatory changes, and technological advancements. By exploring multiple plausible futures, project managers can identify potential risks and develop strategies to address them. Scenario planning is particularly useful for long-term projects with significant external dependencies.

Each of these techniques offers unique insights and advantages, making them valuable tools in the risk assessment process. By employing a combination of these methods, project managers can achieve a more comprehensive understanding of potential risks, enabling more effective mitigation strategies and ultimately enhancing the likelihood of project success. Leveraging these techniques within a hybrid project management framework allows for greater flexibility and adaptability, ensuring that risks are managed proactively throughout the project lifecycle.

Mitigation Strategies

Mitigation strategies in the context of implementing hybrid project management approaches necessitate a thorough understanding of both predictive (traditional) and adaptive (agile) methodologies. The integration of these approaches introduces complexities that require proactive risk management to ensure project success. This chapter delineates several critical strategies that can be employed to mitigate risks inherent in hybrid project environments.

One fundamental strategy is the establishment of a robust risk management framework. This involves identifying potential risks at the outset of the project and continuously monitoring them throughout the project lifecycle. Risk identification should leverage both qualitative and quantitative techniques, such as SWOT analysis (Strengths, Weaknesses, Opportunities, Threats) and Monte Carlo simulations, to provide a comprehensive risk profile. By maintaining a dynamic risk register, project managers can prioritize risks based on their potential impact and likelihood, enabling the allocation of resources to address the most significant threats.

Another key strategy is the implementation of iterative planning and review cycles. Hybrid projects benefit from the adaptability of agile methodologies, which emphasize short, iterative cycles known as sprints. By incorporating regular review points, project teams can assess progress, identify emerging risks, and make necessary adjustments to the project plan. This iterative approach facilitates early detection of issues and allows for timely corrective actions, thereby reducing the probability of project derailment.

Effective communication is paramount in mitigating risks within hybrid projects. The convergence of different project management philosophies can lead to misunderstandings and misalignments among team members. To counteract this, establishing clear communication channels and protocols is essential. Regular status meetings, transparent reporting mechanisms, and the use of collaborative tools can enhance information flow and ensure that all stakeholders are informed about project developments. Additionally, fostering a culture of open communication encourages team members to voice concerns and share insights, which can preempt potential issues.

Stakeholder engagement is another critical component of risk mitigation. Hybrid projects often involve diverse stakeholder groups with varying expectations and interests. Early and continuous engagement with stakeholders helps to align their expectations with project objectives and fosters a sense of ownership and commitment. Techniques such as stakeholder mapping and analysis can identify key stakeholders and their influence on the project. Regular updates, feedback sessions, and involvement in decision-making processes can further strengthen stakeholder relationships and mitigate the risk of resistance or dissatisfaction.

Resource management also plays a pivotal role in mitigating risks. Hybrid projects require a careful balance of resources to accommodate the demands of both predictive and adaptive tasks. Ensuring that team members possess the necessary skills and competencies is crucial. This may involve targeted training programs to upskill team members in agile practices or cross-functional collaboration. Additionally, resource allocation should be flexible to respond to changing project needs, with contingency plans in place to address resource shortages or surpluses.

Lastly, the adoption of appropriate project management tools and technologies can significantly enhance risk mitigation efforts. Tools that support hybrid methodologies, such as integrated project management software, can provide real-time visibility into project status, facilitate collaboration, and automate routine tasks. These tools can also offer advanced analytics and reporting capabilities, enabling project managers to make data-driven decisions and anticipate potential risks.

In summary, the successful implementation of hybrid project management approaches hinges on the effective deployment of mitigation strategies. By establishing a robust risk management framework, incorporating iterative planning and review cycles, fostering effective communication, engaging stakeholders, managing resources adeptly, and leveraging appropriate tools and technologies, project managers can navigate the complexities of hybrid projects and enhance the likelihood of achieving project objectives.

Crisis Management

Effective crisis management is a critical component in the successful implementation of hybrid project management approaches. Hybrid project management combines traditional and agile methodologies to leverage the strengths of both, providing a flexible and robust framework that can adapt to changing circumstances. However, crises can still arise, and organizations must be prepared to address them swiftly and efficiently.

An essential first step in crisis management within hybrid project management is the identification and assessment of potential risks. Comprehensive risk assessment involves identifying possible crisis scenarios, evaluating their likelihood, and determining their potential impact on the project. This can be accomplished through techniques such as SWOT analysis (Strengths, Weaknesses, Opportunities, Threats) and PESTLE analysis (Political, Economic, Social, Technological, Legal, Environmental). By systematically assessing these factors, project teams can prioritize risks and develop tailored response strategies.

Once risks are identified, establishing a crisis management plan is imperative. This plan should outline specific procedures for addressing various types of crises, including communication protocols, roles and responsibilities, and contingency plans. It is crucial to involve all relevant stakeholders in the development of this plan to ensure that it is comprehensive and that everyone understands their role in crisis response. Regular training and simulations can help reinforce these protocols and ensure that the team is prepared for real-world scenarios.

Communication is a pivotal element in crisis management. In a hybrid project environment, where team members may be distributed across various locations and working under different methodologies, maintaining clear and consistent communication is paramount. Establishing a centralized communication hub, such as a dedicated crisis management platform, can facilitate real-time information sharing and coordination. This platform should be accessible to all team members and stakeholders, enabling them to receive updates, share information, and collaborate effectively during a crisis.

Flexibility and adaptability are inherent advantages of hybrid project management and should be leveraged during a crisis. Agile methodologies, with their iterative processes and emphasis on continuous improvement, can be particularly beneficial in responding to rapidly evolving situations. Teams should be encouraged to adapt their plans and processes as new information becomes available, using agile principles such as sprints, stand-ups, and retrospectives to reassess and realign their efforts.

Leadership plays a crucial role in crisis management. Strong, decisive leadership can help maintain team morale and focus during challenging times. Project leaders should exhibit transparency, providing regular updates and being open about the challenges and uncertainties faced. They should also foster a culture of resilience, encouraging team members to remain adaptable and solution-oriented.

Post-crisis analysis is an often-overlooked but vital component of effective crisis management. Once the immediate crisis has been resolved, conducting a thorough review can provide valuable insights into what worked well and what areas need improvement. This analysis should involve all stakeholders and consider both the effectiveness of the crisis response and the impact on project outcomes. Lessons learned should be documented and integrated into future risk management and crisis response plans.

Incorporating these strategies into a hybrid project management framework can enhance an organization's ability to manage crises effectively. By identifying risks, establishing a robust crisis management plan, maintaining clear communication, leveraging the flexibility of hybrid methodologies, demonstrating strong leadership, and conducting post-crisis analysis, organizations can navigate crises more effectively and ensure the successful completion of their projects.

Chapter 10: Performance Measurement and Metrics

Key Performance Indicators (KPIs)

Key performance indicators (KPIs) serve as vital metrics for assessing the efficacy of hybrid project management approaches. Their role is to provide quantifiable data that can be analyzed to determine the success or failure of specific project elements, thus enabling data-driven decision-making. By integrating traditional and agile methodologies, hybrid approaches necessitate a comprehensive framework of KPIs to ensure that both sequential and iterative processes are optimized.

In the context of hybrid project management, KPIs must be meticulously selected to reflect the multifaceted nature of the approach. For instance, traditional KPIs such as schedule variance (SV) and cost performance index (CPI) remain pertinent for assessing the linear aspects of the project. SV measures the degree to which the project is ahead or behind the planned schedule, while CPI evaluates cost efficiency by comparing the budgeted cost of work performed to the actual cost. These metrics provide a foundational understanding of project health from a traditional standpoint.

Conversely, agile-specific KPIs must also be incorporated to capture the iterative and flexible components of the hybrid methodology. Examples include velocity, which measures the amount of work completed in a given iteration, and sprint burndown charts, which track the progress of tasks over time. These metrics are crucial for monitoring the adaptive elements of the project, ensuring that iterative cycles are productive and on track.

The integration of these diverse KPIs requires a balanced approach to avoid conflicts and ensure coherence. One effective strategy is the use of a balanced scorecard, which provides a holistic view by categorizing KPIs into four perspectives: financial, customer, internal process, and learning and growth. This multidimensional framework ensures that all critical aspects of the project are monitored, facilitating a more comprehensive assessment.

Moreover, real-time data collection and analysis are indispensable for the effective utilization of KPIs in hybrid project management. Advanced project management software can be employed to automate the collection of KPI data, enabling real-time dashboards that provide instant insights into project performance. This immediacy allows project managers to make timely adjustments, thereby enhancing the responsiveness of the hybrid approach.

Stakeholder engagement is another crucial factor in the successful implementation of KPIs. Regular communication with stakeholders ensures that KPI metrics align with their expectations and project objectives. This alignment not only fosters stakeholder buy-in but also enhances the relevance and accuracy of the KPIs.

Furthermore, the dynamic nature of hybrid projects necessitates periodic reviews and adjustments of KPIs. As projects evolve, initial KPIs may become obsolete or require refinement. Regular reviews ensure that KPIs remain aligned with the project's changing scope and objectives, thereby maintaining their efficacy throughout the project lifecycle.

The selection and implementation of KPIs in hybrid project management also benefit from a rigorous methodological approach. Techniques such as the SMART criteria (Specific, Measurable, Achievable, Relevant, Time-bound) can be applied to ensure the KPIs are well-defined and actionable. This methodological rigor enhances the reliability and validity of the KPIs, thereby improving their utility in project evaluation.

In summary, KPIs are indispensable tools for the effective management of hybrid projects. Their strategic selection, real-time monitoring, stakeholder alignment, and periodic review ensure that both traditional and agile components are optimized, thereby enhancing overall project performance. The integration of advanced project management tools further augments the efficacy of KPIs, providing project managers with the insights needed to navigate the complexities of hybrid methodologies successfully.

Measuring Success in Hybrid Projects

In the realm of hybrid project management, the evaluation of success necessitates a nuanced understanding that integrates both traditional and agile methodologies. The metrics and parameters used to measure success must be adaptable to the diverse nature of hybrid projects, which often encompass a mixture of predictive and adaptive elements. This subchapter delves into the critical dimensions for assessing the success of hybrid projects, highlighting key performance indicators (KPIs), stakeholder satisfaction, and the achievement of project objectives.

Key performance indicators (KPIs) serve as the cornerstone for measuring success in hybrid projects. These indicators should be carefully selected to reflect the dual nature of hybrid methodologies. Traditional KPIs, such as adherence to budget, schedule compliance, and scope realization, remain relevant. However, it is equally important to incorporate agile-specific KPIs, such as velocity, iteration burndown, and team adaptability. The integration of these diverse metrics provides a comprehensive view of project performance, enabling project managers to monitor progress and make informed decisions.

Stakeholder satisfaction is another pivotal dimension in evaluating the success of hybrid projects. Given the dynamic nature of hybrid methodologies, continuous engagement with stakeholders is essential. Regular feedback loops, facilitated through agile practices like sprint reviews and retrospectives, ensure that stakeholder expectations are met and any necessary adjustments are promptly addressed. Quantitative measures, such as Net Promoter Score (NPS) and Customer Satisfaction (CSAT) scores, can be employed to gauge stakeholder contentment. Additionally, qualitative feedback should be systematically gathered and analyzed to capture insights that may not be immediately apparent through numerical data.

Achievement of project objectives is fundamentally tied to the success of hybrid projects. These objectives should be clearly defined at the outset and revisited throughout the project lifecycle. The hybrid approach allows for flexibility in adjusting objectives as the project evolves, thus aligning with both long term strategic goals and short-term tactical needs. Milestone reviews and performance assessments are instrumental in tracking the attainment of these objectives. Employing a balanced scorecard approach can help in aligning project deliverables with organizational goals, ensuring a holistic evaluation of success.

Risk management is an integral aspect of measuring success in hybrid projects. The hybrid model inherently involves a higher degree of uncertainty due to its adaptive components. Effective risk management strategies, including risk identification, assessment, and mitigation, are crucial. The use of risk-adjusted performance metrics can provide a more accurate representation of project health. For instance, incorporating risk-adjusted return on investment (ROI) and earned value management (EVM) can offer insights into project performance relative to the inherent risks.

The human factor cannot be overlooked in the measurement of success. Team performance and morale are significant indicators of a project's health. Hybrid projects often require a high degree of collaboration and adaptability among team members. Metrics such as team satisfaction, collaboration efficiency, and innovation rate can offer valuable insights into the human dynamics of the project. Regular team assessments and fostering a culture of continuous improvement are essential for maintaining high performance and morale.

Incorporating these multifaceted dimensions into the evaluation framework ensures a robust and comprehensive assessment of hybrid project success. The dynamic interplay between traditional and agile metrics, stakeholder satisfaction, objective achievement, risk management, and human factors creates a holistic view that is essential for the nuanced nature of hybrid project management.

Continuous Improvement

Continuous improvement within the framework of hybrid project management is a critical element for achieving sustained project success. This concept, deeply rooted in methodologies such as Lean and Six Sigma, emphasizes the importance of iterative enhancements and incremental progress. When applying a hybrid approach, continuous improvement necessitates a strategic blend of agile flexibility and traditional project management rigor.

Central to continuous improvement is the Plan-Do-Check-Act (PDCA) cycle, a time-tested model that fosters a systematic approach to problem-solving and process optimization. In the context of hybrid project management, the PDCA cycle can be seamlessly integrated to ensure that both adaptive and predictive elements of the project are continually refined. During the planning phase, project teams must identify key performance metrics and establish benchmarks that align with strategic objectives. These metrics should encompass both agile-specific indicators, such as sprint velocity and burn-down rates, and traditional metrics like earned value and schedule variance.

The execution phase, or 'Do', involves the implementation of the project plan while maintaining a vigilant focus on real-time data and feedback. Hybrid project teams are encouraged to conduct frequent retrospectives and reviews, akin to agile sprint reviews, to assess progress and identify areas for improvement. These sessions should be structured to facilitate open communication and foster a culture of continuous learning and adaptation.

The 'Check' phase is critical for measuring the effectiveness of the implemented changes. This involves rigorous data analysis and performance evaluation against the predefined metrics. Advanced analytical tools and techniques, such as statistical process control (SPC) and root cause analysis (RCA), can be employed to gain deeper insights into project performance and identify underlying issues. The hybrid approach benefits from the agility of continuous feedback loops, enabling teams to pivot and make necessary adjustments swiftly.

The final 'Act' phase focuses on standardizing successful practices and implementing corrective actions for any identified deficiencies. This phase is characterized by documenting lessons learned, updating process documentation, and refining best practices. In a hybrid project environment, this often translates to a dynamic repository of knowledge that evolves with each iteration, ensuring that improvements are institutionalized and disseminated across the organization.

Moreover, leveraging technology and automation can significantly enhance the continuous improvement process in hybrid projects. Project management software and collaboration tools can streamline data collection, facilitate real-time communication, and provide robust analytics capabilities. These tools enable project teams to maintain a holistic view of project performance and make data-driven decisions that drive continuous improvement.

Another critical aspect is fostering a culture that values and rewards continuous improvement. Leadership plays a pivotal role in this regard, as they must champion the principles of continuous improvement and create an environment where team members feel empowered to innovate and experiment. Training and development programs focused on Lean, Six Sigma, and agile methodologies can equip team members with the necessary skills and knowledge to contribute effectively to the continuous improvement process.

In the hybrid project management paradigm, continuous improvement is not a one-time initiative but an ongoing commitment to excellence. By integrating the PDCA cycle, leveraging technology, and fostering a supportive culture, organizations can achieve a state of perpetual enhancement, ultimately leading to more successful project outcomes and a sustained competitive advantage.

Reporting and Documentation

Effective reporting and documentation are paramount in the successful implementation of a hybrid project management approach. The integration of traditional and agile methodologies necessitates an adaptable yet structured framework for tracking progress, recording decisions, and communicating with stakeholders. This subchapter delineates the critical components and best practices for reporting and documentation in hybrid project environments.

A comprehensive reporting system in a hybrid project must cater to the diverse needs of stakeholders, ranging from detailed progress reports for project managers to high-level summaries for executive sponsors. Traditional project management often relies on periodic status reports, Gantt charts, and earned value management (EVM) metrics to monitor progress. In contrast, agile methodologies emphasize iterative progress through burndown charts, sprint reviews, and retrospective meetings. The hybrid approach leverages the strengths of both systems by incorporating structured periodic reporting while maintaining the flexibility of agile feedback loops.

Centralized documentation is another cornerstone of hybrid project management. Documentation serves as the repository of all project-related information, including scope statements, risk registers, change logs, and meeting minutes. Effective documentation ensures transparency, accountability, and continuity, particularly in complex projects involving multiple teams and phases. Hybrid projects benefit from a dynamic documentation system that can be updated in real-time to reflect ongoing changes and iterations.

Key to successful hybrid reporting and documentation is the use of appropriate tools and technologies. Project management software that supports both traditional and agile methodologies can streamline the documentation process and facilitate seamless integration of reporting mechanisms. Tools such as Microsoft Project, Jira, and Trello offer functionalities that cater to hybrid needs, enabling project managers to create customized dashboards, track progress across different methodologies, and generate comprehensive reports.

Standardization of reporting formats and documentation templates is crucial for consistency and clarity. Establishing standardized templates for progress reports, risk assessments, and change requests helps in maintaining uniformity across the project lifecycle. These templates should be flexible enough to accommodate the unique requirements of both traditional and agile components of the project. For instance, a hybrid project status report might include sections for Gantt chart milestones as well as sprint achievements and upcoming iterations.

Regular communication with stakeholders is facilitated through structured reporting schedules and documentation reviews. Stakeholder engagement is critical in hybrid projects, where changes and iterations are frequent. Scheduled reporting intervals, such as bi-weekly status meetings and monthly executive briefings, ensure that stakeholders are kept informed of progress, risks, and any deviations from the project plan. Documentation reviews, including formal sign-offs on key deliverables and change requests, provide checkpoints for validating project alignment with objectives.

The role of the project manager in a hybrid environment extends to ensuring the integrity and accuracy of all reports and documentation. This includes verifying data accuracy, updating records promptly, and ensuring that all team members adhere to documentation standards. The project manager must also facilitate collaboration among team members to ensure that documentation reflects the collective input and insights of the entire project team.

In hybrid project management, the iterative nature of agile practices requires a continuous feedback loop for reporting and documentation. Regular retrospective meetings and sprint reviews offer opportunities to assess the effectiveness of current reporting practices and identify areas for improvement. Incorporating feedback into the documentation process ensures that it evolves in line with project needs and stakeholder expectations.

In conclusion, effective reporting and documentation in hybrid project management are critical to ensuring project success. By integrating the rigor of traditional methodologies with the flexibility of agile practices, project managers can create a robust framework that supports transparency, accountability, and continuous improvement.

Chapter 11: Technology and Tools

Project Management Software

The evolution of project management methodologies has seen a significant shift from traditional approaches to more flexible and adaptive strategies. This transformation is largely driven by the need to address complex project environments that are characterized by rapid changes and uncertainties. One of the critical enablers of this evolution is the development and integration of project management software, which provides robust support for planning, executing, and monitoring projects.

Project management software serves as a comprehensive tool that bridges the gap between theoretical methodologies and practical application. It offers a suite of features designed to enhance collaboration, streamline processes, and improve overall project efficiency. Key functionalities typically include task scheduling, resource allocation, time tracking, budget management, and risk assessment. These features are essential for maintaining control over project variables and ensuring that objectives are met within the defined constraints.

The adoption of project management software is particularly advantageous in hybrid project management approaches, which blend elements of traditional and agile methodologies. This hybrid model leverages the structured planning and control mechanisms of traditional project management while incorporating the flexibility and iterative processes characteristic of agile practices. Project management software facilitates this integration by providing tools that support both linear and iterative workflows.

One of the primary benefits of using project management software in a hybrid approach is the ability to maintain a high level of transparency and visibility across all project phases. Real-time data updates and dashboards enable project managers and stakeholders to monitor progress, identify potential issues, and make informed decisions promptly. This level of insight is crucial for managing the dynamic and often unpredictable nature of hybrid projects.

Collaboration is another area where project management software excels. By offering centralized platforms for communication and document sharing, these tools foster a collaborative environment where team members can work together seamlessly, regardless of their geographical locations. Features such as discussion boards, file sharing, and integrated messaging systems ensure that all team members are aligned and informed, reducing the risk of miscommunication and enhancing overall project cohesion.

Resource management is a critical aspect of project execution, and project management software provides sophisticated tools to optimize the utilization of resources. These tools allow project managers to allocate resources effectively, track their usage, and adjust assignments as needed to address changing project demands. This capability is particularly important in hybrid projects, where resource requirements may fluctuate due to the iterative nature of agile practices.

Risk management is another domain where project management software proves invaluable. By providing risk assessment and mitigation tools, these platforms enable project managers to identify potential risks early in the project lifecycle and develop strategies to address them. This proactive approach to risk management helps in minimizing the impact of unforeseen events and ensures that projects stay on track.

In addition to these core functionalities, many project management software solutions offer advanced features such as automation, artificial intelligence, and machine learning. These technologies enhance the predictive capabilities of the software, allowing for more accurate forecasting and decision-making. Automation can streamline repetitive tasks, freeing up valuable time for project managers to focus on strategic planning and problem-solving.

The integration of project management software into hybrid project management approaches represents a significant advancement in the field. By providing a comprehensive and adaptable toolset, these platforms enable project managers to navigate the complexities of modern projects with greater efficiency and effectiveness. The continuous evolution of project management software promises to further enhance its capabilities, driving innovation and improving outcomes in the realm of project management.

Collaboration Tools

Effective project management often necessitates the integration of various collaboration tools to streamline communication, enhance productivity, and ensure the seamless execution of tasks. The hybrid approach, which combines elements of both traditional and agile methodologies, significantly benefits from the strategic use of these tools. The choice and implementation of appropriate collaboration tools are critical in managing complex projects that require the alignment of diverse teams and stakeholders.

Central to the hybrid approach is the need for real-time communication and the facilitation of efficient information sharing. Tools such as Slack, Microsoft Teams, and Zoom have become indispensable in this context. These platforms enable instant messaging, video conferencing, and file sharing, which are essential for maintaining continuous dialogue and fostering a collaborative environment. The integration of these tools ensures that team members, regardless of their geographical location, can participate actively and contribute to the project's progress.

Project management software like Asana, Trello, and Jira is pivotal in organizing tasks, tracking progress, and managing workflows. These tools support the hybrid approach by offering features that cater to both agile and traditional project management practices. For instance, Jira's Kanban boards are ideal for agile sprints, while its Gantt chart functionalities support more traditional, timeline-based planning. This dual capability allows project managers to tailor their approach based on the project's specific needs, thereby optimizing resource allocation and task prioritization.

Document management systems such as Google Workspace and Microsoft Office 365 play a crucial role in ensuring that all project documentation is accessible, up-to-date, and secure. These platforms offer collaborative editing features, version control, and cloud storage, which are vital for maintaining the integrity and availability of project documents. The ability to track changes and manage document versions mitigates the risk of errors and ensures that all team members are working with the most current information.

Furthermore, collaboration tools that integrate with each other create a cohesive ecosystem that enhances overall project efficiency. For example, the integration of Slack with Google Drive or Trello allows for seamless file sharing and task management within a single communication thread. This interconnectedness reduces the need for constant switching between different applications, thereby saving time and minimizing disruptions.

The hybrid approach also benefits from tools that facilitate stakeholder engagement and feedback. Platforms such as Miro and MURAL offer virtual whiteboard capabilities, enabling interactive brainstorming sessions and collaborative planning. These tools are particularly useful for remote teams, as they replicate the experience of in-person meetings and workshops, fostering creative problem-solving and idea generation.

Security and compliance are paramount considerations when selecting collaboration tools. Ensuring that the chosen platforms adhere to industry standards and regulations, such as GDPR or HIPAA, is essential for protecting sensitive project data. Features like end-to-end encryption, multi-factor authentication, and audit logs enhance the security posture of collaboration tools, thereby safeguarding the project's integrity.

Incorporating collaboration tools into the hybrid project management framework requires careful planning and consideration. Project managers must assess the specific needs of their teams, the complexity of the project, and the existing technological infrastructure. Training and support are also critical to ensure that team members are proficient in using the selected tools, thereby maximizing their potential benefits.

The strategic implementation of collaboration tools within the hybrid approach not only enhances communication and productivity but also aligns with the dynamic nature of modern project management. By leveraging these tools effectively, project managers can navigate the complexities of their projects, ensuring successful outcomes and the achievement of project objectives.

Data Analytics and Reporting Tools

Data analytics and reporting tools play a pivotal role in the effective implementation of a hybrid approach in project management. These tools facilitate the collection, analysis, and interpretation of data, which are essential for informed decision-making and successful project execution. The integration of data analytics into project management allows for real-time monitoring, predictive analysis, and comprehensive reporting, thereby enhancing the overall efficiency and effectiveness of project management processes.

One of the primary benefits of utilizing data analytics in a hybrid project management approach is the ability to monitor project performance in real-time. Real-time data collection and analysis enable project managers to identify potential issues and bottlenecks early in the project lifecycle. This proactive approach allows for timely interventions, thereby reducing the risk of project delays and cost overruns. Tools such as dashboards and performance metrics provide a visual representation of project status, making it easier for stakeholders to understand the current state of the project and make informed decisions.

Predictive analytics is another significant advantage offered by data analytics tools. By leveraging historical project data, predictive analytics can forecast future project performance and outcomes. This capability is particularly useful in a hybrid approach, where both agile and traditional project management methodologies are employed. Predictive analytics can help project managers anticipate potential risks and challenges, allowing them to develop contingency plans and allocate resources more effectively. Additionally, predictive analytics can identify patterns and trends that may not be immediately apparent, providing valuable insights that can inform strategic decision-making.

Comprehensive reporting is a critical component of effective project management. Data analytics tools enable the generation of detailed reports that provide a holistic view of project performance. These reports can include key performance indicators (KPIs), progress updates, risk assessments, and financial summaries. The ability to generate customized reports tailored to the specific needs of different stakeholders ensures that relevant information is communicated clearly and concisely. This transparency fosters better collaboration and alignment among project team members and stakeholders.

Several data analytics and reporting tools are commonly used in the implementation of a hybrid project management approach. Tools such as Microsoft Power BI, Tableau, and Google Data Studio offer robust data visualization and reporting capabilities. These tools enable project managers to create interactive dashboards and detailed reports that can be easily shared with stakeholders. Additionally, project management software such as Jira, Asana, and Trello often include built-in analytics and reporting features, further streamlining the data collection and analysis process.

The integration of data analytics and reporting tools into a hybrid project management approach also supports continuous improvement. By analyzing project data, organizations can identify areas for improvement and implement changes to enhance future project performance. This iterative process of data-driven decision-making and continuous improvement aligns with the principles of both agile and traditional project management methodologies, making it well-suited to a hybrid approach.

Incorporating data analytics and reporting tools into a hybrid project management approach requires careful planning and execution. It is essential to select the right tools that align with the organization's needs and project requirements. Additionally, project managers and team members must be trained to effectively use these tools and interpret the data they generate. Establishing clear processes for data collection, analysis, and reporting is also critical to ensure that the insights gained from data analytics are actionable and contribute to the successful implementation of the project.

Data analytics and reporting tools are indispensable for the successful implementation of a hybrid project management approach. They provide the necessary insights and visibility to make informed decisions, anticipate and mitigate risks, and continuously improve project performance. By leveraging these tools, organizations can enhance their project management capabilities and achieve better project outcomes.

Emerging Technologies

Emerging technologies are revolutionizing the landscape of project management by offering innovative tools and methodologies that enhance efficiency, accuracy, and adaptability. The integration of these technologies into a hybrid project management approach can yield significant benefits, such as improved decision-making, real-time data analysis, and seamless collaboration among stakeholders.

Artificial Intelligence (AI) and Machine Learning (ML) are at the forefront of these advancements. AI algorithms can process vast amounts of data to identify patterns and predict project outcomes, enabling project managers to make informed decisions. ML models can continuously learn from project data, optimizing resource allocation and risk management. For instance, predictive analytics can forecast potential delays and budget overruns, allowing teams to proactively address issues.

Blockchain technology is another emerging tool with the potential to transform project management. By providing a decentralized and immutable ledger, blockchain ensures transparency and security in project transactions. Smart contracts, which are self-executing contracts with the terms directly written into code, can automate and enforce agreements, reducing the need for intermediaries and minimizing the risk of disputes. This technology is particularly valuable in projects involving multiple parties, where trust and accountability are paramount.

The Internet of Things (IoT) is expanding the scope of data collection and monitoring in project environments. IoT devices can gather real-time data on various project parameters, such as equipment performance, environmental conditions, and workforce productivity. This data can be integrated into project management software to provide a comprehensive view of the project's status, facilitating timely interventions and adjustments. For example, in construction projects, IoT sensors can monitor structural integrity and environmental factors, ensuring safety and compliance with regulations.

Virtual Reality (VR) and Augmented Reality (AR) are enhancing visualization and collaboration in project management. VR can create immersive simulations of project environments, allowing stakeholders to experience and evaluate designs before implementation. AR overlays digital information onto the physical world, enabling on-site personnel to access critical data and instructions in real-time. These technologies can improve communication and reduce misunderstandings, particularly in complex projects that require precise coordination.

The adoption of cloud computing is also reshaping project management practices. Cloud-based platforms offer scalable and flexible solutions for data storage, processing, and collaboration. Project management software hosted on the cloud allows teams to access and update project information from anywhere, fostering remote work and global collaboration. The cloud's ability to handle large datasets and support advanced analytics further enhances project planning and execution.

Robotic Process Automation (RPA) is streamlining repetitive and time-consuming tasks in project management. RPA software robots can automate activities such as data entry, report generation, and compliance checks, freeing up human resources for more strategic functions. This automation reduces the risk of errors and accelerates project workflows, contributing to overall efficiency.

The integration of these emerging technologies into a hybrid project management approach requires a strategic framework that aligns technological capabilities with project objectives. Organizations need to invest in training and development to equip their teams with the necessary skills to leverage these tools effectively. Additionally, a robust IT infrastructure and data governance policies are essential to ensure the reliability and security of technological implementations.

As these technologies continue to evolve, their impact on project management will likely grow, offering new opportunities for innovation and improvement. By staying abreast of technological advancements and adopting a hybrid approach, organizations can enhance their project management practices and achieve greater success in an increasingly complex and dynamic environment.

Chapter 12: Case Studies and Real-World Examples

Successful Hybrid Projects

In today's dynamic business environment, the hybrid project management approach has emerged as a pivotal strategy for ensuring the successful completion of complex projects. This approach leverages the strengths of both traditional and agile methodologies, allowing project managers to tailor their processes to the unique demands of each project. The hybrid approach offers a flexible framework that combines the structured planning and control of traditional project management with the adaptability and iterative progress of agile methods.

Central to the success of hybrid projects is the careful selection and integration of methodologies. Project managers must assess the project's requirements, stakeholder expectations, and organizational context to determine the most appropriate blend of practices. For instance, the traditional Waterfall model may be suitable for well-defined project phases with clear deliverables, while agile practices like Scrum or Kanban can be integrated for tasks requiring iterative development and frequent feedback loops.

Effective communication and collaboration are crucial components of successful hybrid projects. Establishing clear communication channels and fostering a collaborative environment ensures that all team members are aligned with the project goals and can adapt to changes swiftly. Regular meetings, progress updates, and feedback sessions help maintain transparency and keep the project on track. Additionally, involving stakeholders throughout the project lifecycle enhances their engagement and ensures that the final deliverables meet their expectations.

Resource management is another critical factor in hybrid project success. Project managers need to allocate resources efficiently, balancing the demands of different project phases and ensuring that team members have the necessary skills and tools to perform their tasks effectively. This may involve cross-training team members, leveraging external expertise, or utilizing project management software to streamline resource allocation and tracking.

Risk management is also integral to the hybrid approach. By combining predictive and adaptive strategies, project managers can identify potential risks early and develop contingency plans to mitigate them. Traditional risk management techniques, such as risk assessment matrices and mitigation plans, can be complemented by agile practices like regular retrospectives and sprint reviews, which allow teams to address issues promptly and adjust their strategies as needed.

The hybrid approach also emphasizes continuous improvement and learning. Project managers should encourage a culture of reflection and feedback, where team members can learn from their experiences and apply these lessons to future projects. This can be facilitated through post-project reviews, lessons learned sessions, and the incorporation of best practices into organizational processes.

Technology plays a significant role in the successful implementation of hybrid projects. Utilizing project management tools that support both traditional and agile methodologies can streamline workflows, enhance communication, and provide real-time visibility into project progress. These tools can help project managers track milestones, manage tasks, and monitor resource utilization, ensuring that the project remains on schedule and within budget.

In essence, the hybrid approach to project management offers a versatile and effective framework for navigating the complexities of modern projects. By strategically integrating traditional and agile practices, fostering effective communication and collaboration, managing resources and risks efficiently, emphasizing continuous improvement, and leveraging technology, project managers can enhance their ability to deliver successful project outcomes.

Lessons Learned

The application of a hybrid project management approach offers a synthesis of traditional and agile methodologies, aiming to leverage the strengths of both to enhance project outcomes. This subchapter delineates the critical insights gained from implementing such an approach across various project scenarios.

One of the primary observations is the necessity of a balanced integration between agile flexibility and the structured predictability of traditional methods. Projects that managed to achieve this balance reported higher success rates in terms of meeting deadlines, staying within budget, and delivering anticipated quality. The hybrid approach facilitated adaptive planning and iterative progress, which proved particularly beneficial in dynamic environments where requirements frequently evolved. Conversely, the traditional elements provided a robust framework for risk management and resource allocation.

Another significant lesson pertains to stakeholder engagement. The hybrid model necessitates a more nuanced approach to communication. Agile practices advocate for continuous stakeholder involvement and feedback, which can sometimes conflict with the more formal communication channels of traditional project management. Successful projects developed a dual communication strategy that incorporated regular, informal updates alongside formal reporting mechanisms. This duality ensured that stakeholders remained informed and engaged without overwhelming them with excessive information.

Team dynamics also emerged as a critical factor. Hybrid projects often require teams to shift between agile and traditional mindsets, which can be challenging. Effective hybrid implementations invested in comprehensive training programs that equipped team members with the skills needed to operate within both paradigms. Additionally, fostering a culture of flexibility and continuous learning was essential. Teams that embraced these values were better able to navigate the complexities of a hybrid approach, leading to more cohesive and productive work environments.

Resource management in hybrid projects revealed another set of insights. The iterative nature of agile practices can sometimes lead to resource contention, especially when juxtaposed with the fixed schedules of traditional methods. Projects that successfully mitigated this issue employed dynamic resource allocation strategies, allowing resources to be reallocated based on real-time project needs. This approach required robust monitoring tools and a proactive management style to ensure resources were optimally utilized.

The hybrid approach also highlighted the importance of tailored methodologies. One-size-fits-all solutions were less effective than customized strategies that considered the unique aspects of each project. Projects that took the time to assess their specific needs and constraints before selecting the elements of agile and traditional methodologies to combine saw better outcomes. This customization often involved pilot testing different hybrid configurations before full-scale implementation, allowing for adjustments based on empirical evidence.

Risk management in hybrid projects benefited from the dual approach as well. The predictive nature of traditional risk management techniques was complemented by the responsive capabilities of agile practices. This combination allowed for a more comprehensive risk management strategy that could address both anticipated and emergent risks. Projects that integrated risk management practices from both methodologies were better equipped to handle uncertainties and disruptions.

The lessons learned from applying a hybrid approach to project management underscore the need for adaptability, strategic communication, and a deep understanding of both agile and traditional methodologies. By synthesizing these insights, organizations can better navigate the complexities of modern project environments, ultimately leading to improved project performance and outcomes.

Industry-Specific Applications

The integration of hybrid approaches in project implementation has seen a marked increase across various industries, each leveraging the flexibility and robustness of hybrid methodologies to meet specific sector demands. This section delineates how hybrid approaches are tailored and applied within different industrial contexts, providing a comprehensive understanding of their versatility and effectiveness.

In the construction industry, hybrid project management methodologies amalgamate traditional Waterfall models with Agile practices to address the sector's unique requirements. Construction projects often involve extensive planning and design phases, necessitating a sequential approach for initial stages. However, the implementation phase can benefit significantly from Agile practices, which allow for iterative development and quick adjustments in response to unforeseen challenges. For instance, while the architectural design might follow a Waterfall approach, the actual construction can employ Agile sprints to ensure adaptability and responsiveness to on-site issues, thus enhancing project efficiency and reducing delays.

Within the realm of information technology (IT), hybrid approaches are particularly beneficial. IT projects often require a balance between structured frameworks and the need for rapid iteration due to the fast-paced nature of technological advancements. A hybrid approach can integrate the comprehensive planning and risk assessment of the Waterfall model with the flexibility and customer-centric focus of Agile methodologies. This duality ensures that IT projects, such as software development or system integrations, maintain a clear roadmap while remaining adaptable to evolving requirements and stakeholder feedback.

Healthcare industry projects also benefit from hybrid methodologies, especially in the development and implementation of health information systems. These projects demand high levels of precision and compliance with regulatory standards, which are well-suited to the structured aspects of the Waterfall approach. Concurrently, the iterative and incremental nature of Agile methods allows for continuous user involvement and feedback, which is crucial in developing systems that meet the practical needs of healthcare professionals. This combination ensures that projects are both compliant and user-friendly, ultimately enhancing patient care and operational efficiency.

In the financial services sector, hybrid approaches are employed to manage the development and deployment of complex financial products and services. The stringent regulatory environment necessitates a thorough planning phase, characteristic of the Waterfall methodology. However, the competitive and dynamic market conditions require the agility to pivot and adapt quickly, for which Agile practices are indispensable. By integrating these methodologies, financial institutions can maintain compliance while innovating and responding promptly to market changes and customer demands.

Manufacturing industries leverage hybrid approaches to streamline production processes and enhance product development cycles. The initial stages of product design and development often follow a Waterfall approach to ensure comprehensive planning and risk management. As the project transitions to the production phase, Agile methodologies facilitate iterative improvements and rapid response to production issues. This hybrid model ensures that manufacturing projects benefit from both meticulous planning and operational flexibility, leading to improved product quality and reduced time-to-market.

The education sector also finds value in hybrid project management, particularly in the development and deployment of educational technologies and curriculum redesign projects. The structured planning of Waterfall ensures alignment with educational standards and objectives, while the iterative processes of Agile allow for continuous feedback from educators and students. This ensures that the end products are both pedagogically sound and user-centric, enhancing the overall educational experience.

In summary, the application of hybrid approaches across various industries underscores their adaptability and efficacy in addressing sector-specific challenges. By combining the strengths of traditional and Agile methodologies, organizations can achieve a balanced, responsive, and robust project management framework tailored to their unique needs.

Future Trends

The field of project management has witnessed significant transformations over the past decades, driven by the need for greater efficiency, flexibility, and adaptability. As organizations continue to operate in increasingly complex and dynamic environments, the adoption of hybrid approaches in project management is expected to evolve further. Several key trends are anticipated to shape the future landscape of hybrid project management.

Firstly, the integration of advanced technologies such as artificial intelligence (AI) and machine learning (ML) is poised to revolutionize hybrid project management. These technologies offer the potential to enhance decision-making processes, optimize resource allocation, and predict project outcomes with greater accuracy. AI-driven analytics can provide real-time insights, enabling project managers to identify potential risks and opportunities at an early stage. Machine learning algorithms can be employed to analyze historical project data, uncovering patterns and trends that can inform future project planning and execution.

Another significant trend is the increasing emphasis on data-driven project management. With the proliferation of big data, project managers have access to an unprecedented volume of information. Leveraging this data effectively can lead to more informed decision-making and improved project outcomes. Advanced data analytics tools are expected to become integral components of hybrid project management frameworks, facilitating the extraction of actionable insights from vast datasets. This shift towards data-centric approaches will necessitate the development of new skills and competencies among project managers, including data literacy and analytical capabilities.

The rise of remote and distributed teams is also expected to influence the evolution of hybrid project management. The COVID-19 pandemic has accelerated the adoption of remote work, and this trend is likely to persist in the post-pandemic era. Hybrid project management approaches will need to accommodate the unique challenges and opportunities associated with remote collaboration. Effective communication and collaboration tools, such as virtual workspaces and project management software, will be essential in ensuring seamless coordination among geographically dispersed team members. Additionally, fostering a culture of trust and accountability will be crucial in maintaining team cohesion and productivity in a remote work environment.

Agile methodologies are anticipated to continue playing a pivotal role in hybrid project management. The principles of agility, including iterative development, continuous feedback, and adaptive planning, align well with the dynamic nature of modern projects. Hybrid approaches that incorporate agile elements can provide the flexibility needed to respond to changing project requirements and stakeholder expectations.

However, the challenge lies in balancing agility with the structured processes of traditional project management methodologies. Organizations will need to develop tailored hybrid frameworks that integrate the best practices of both agile and traditional approaches.

Sustainability and environmental considerations are becoming increasingly important in project management. As organizations prioritize corporate social responsibility and sustainable development goals, hybrid project management approaches will need to incorporate sustainability principles. This includes minimizing the environmental impact of projects, promoting resource efficiency, and ensuring long-term viability. Project managers will be expected to adopt green practices and consider the broader social and environmental implications of their projects.

The future of hybrid project management will also be shaped by the evolving role of the project manager. Beyond technical proficiency, project managers will need to develop strong leadership and interpersonal skills. The ability to navigate complex stakeholder relationships, foster collaboration, and drive organizational change will be critical. Continuous professional development and lifelong learning will be essential in equipping project managers with the competencies required to thrive in a rapidly changing landscape.

In conclusion, the future of hybrid project management is characterized by the convergence of advanced technologies, data-driven approaches, remote collaboration, agile methodologies, sustainability considerations, and evolving leadership paradigms. Organizations that proactively adapt to these trends will be better positioned to achieve project success in an increasingly complex and dynamic environment.

Chapter 13: Advantages and Disadvantages

Advantages of Hybrid Approach

The hybrid approach in project management amalgamates the best practices from traditional methodologies, such as Waterfall, and contemporary frameworks like Agile. This synthesis aims to leverage the strengths of each methodology while mitigating their respective weaknesses. The primary advantage of this approach lies in its flexibility and adaptability, which can be instrumental in navigating the complexities and uncertainties inherent in modern projects.

One significant benefit of the hybrid approach is its ability to enhance project planning and execution. Traditional methodologies emphasize thorough upfront planning and well-defined stages, which provide a clear roadmap and detailed documentation. This aspect is particularly advantageous for projects with well-understood requirements and regulatory constraints. However, traditional methods can be rigid and may struggle to accommodate changes. By integrating Agile principles, which prioritize iterative development and flexibility, the hybrid approach allows for adjustments and refinements throughout the project lifecycle. This dual capability ensures that the project remains aligned with evolving stakeholder expectations and market conditions.

Resource optimization is another critical advantage. In traditional project management, resource allocation is often fixed and predetermined, which can lead to inefficiencies if project requirements change. Agile methodologies, on the other hand, promote dynamic resource allocation based on iterative cycles, enabling teams to respond quickly to emerging needs and priorities. The hybrid approach combines these strategies, allowing project managers to allocate resources more effectively and efficiently. This adaptability can result in better utilization of human, financial, and technological resources, ultimately improving project outcomes.

Risk management is enhanced through the hybrid approach. Traditional methodologies typically involve comprehensive risk assessments at the outset, identifying potential issues and devising mitigation strategies. While this is valuable, it can be insufficient for addressing risks that emerge during project execution. Agile practices introduce continuous risk assessment and iterative feedback loops, enabling teams to identify and address risks in real-time. The hybrid approach integrates these practices, providing a robust framework for proactive and reactive risk management. This can significantly reduce the likelihood of project delays and cost overruns, thereby increasing the overall probability of success.

Stakeholder engagement and satisfaction are also positively impacted. Traditional methodologies often involve periodic updates and formal communication channels, which can lead to delays in feedback and decision-making. Agile frameworks promote regular interaction with stakeholders through iterative reviews and collaborative planning sessions. By combining these communication strategies, the hybrid approach ensures that stakeholders are consistently informed and actively involved in the project. This can enhance stakeholder trust and support, fostering a collaborative environment that is conducive to project success.

The hybrid approach also facilitates continuous improvement. Traditional methodologies emphasize post-project reviews and lessons learned, which are valuable for future projects but may not impact the current one. Agile principles focus on ongoing improvement through regular retrospectives and incremental enhancements. By integrating these practices, the hybrid approach enables teams to implement improvements throughout the project lifecycle. This can lead to higher quality deliverables, increased efficiency, and a more positive project experience for all involved.

In conclusion, the hybrid approach in project management offers a multitude of advantages by combining the strengths of traditional and Agile methodologies. Its flexibility, enhanced planning and execution capabilities, efficient resource utilization, robust risk management, improved stakeholder engagement, and commitment to continuous improvement make it a compelling choice for managing complex projects in dynamic environments.

Disadvantages and Challenges

Implementing a hybrid approach in project management, while offering numerous advantages, is not without its downsides and obstacles. One primary challenge is the complexity involved in integrating diverse methodologies. The hybrid approach often necessitates the blending of traditional Waterfall methods with Agile practices, which can lead to complications in terms of workflow synchronization, resource allocation, and timeline management. This complexity can result in increased project management overhead, requiring more sophisticated tools and higher levels of expertise to ensure seamless integration.

Another significant disadvantage is the potential for resistance to change within the organization. Employees accustomed to a single, established methodology may find it difficult to adapt to a hybrid approach. This resistance can stem from a lack of understanding, fear of the unknown, or a perceived increase in workload. Overcoming this resistance often requires comprehensive training programs, which can be time-consuming and costly. Additionally, the success of these training programs is not guaranteed, as they hinge on the willingness and ability of the employees to adapt.

The hybrid approach can also introduce ambiguity in roles and responsibilities. In traditional project management, roles are often clearly defined and static throughout the project lifecycle. However, in a hybrid environment, the fluid nature of Agile practices can blur these lines, leading to confusion and potential conflicts among team members. This ambiguity can hinder effective communication and collaboration, ultimately impacting the project's success.

Resource management presents another challenge. The hybrid approach requires a careful balance of resources to accommodate both Waterfall and Agile components. This balancing act can be particularly difficult in organizations with limited resources, leading to potential resource shortages or overallocation. Moreover, the need for dual expertise in both methodologies can strain the available talent pool, necessitating either the hiring of additional skilled personnel or extensive upskilling of current employees.

The hybrid approach also faces difficulties in maintaining consistency and standardization across projects. Given that different projects may require different blends of methodologies, establishing a consistent framework for project execution can be challenging. This lack of standardization can complicate project monitoring and control, making it harder to measure performance and ensure quality across multiple projects.

Additionally, the hybrid approach can pose challenges in stakeholder management. Stakeholders accustomed to traditional project management may find the iterative and incremental nature of Agile practices disconcerting. This can lead to misaligned expectations, as stakeholders may expect detailed upfront plans and rigid timelines, which are not always feasible in a hybrid environment. Effective communication and continuous stakeholder engagement are crucial to mitigate these issues, but they require significant effort and resources.

Finally, the hybrid approach can impact project scalability. While Agile practices excel in smaller, more flexible projects, scaling these practices to larger, more complex projects can be problematic. The hybrid approach must carefully navigate this scalability issue to ensure that the benefits of both methodologies are realized without compromising the project's overall objectives.

In conclusion, while the hybrid approach offers a promising avenue for enhancing project management, it is not without its drawbacks. Organizations must carefully weigh these disadvantages and challenges against the potential benefits, taking proactive measures to address them. This includes investing in training and development, fostering a culture of adaptability, and implementing robust project management tools and techniques. Only through diligent planning and execution can the hybrid approach be successfully integrated into an organization's project management framework.

Balancing the Pros and Cons

The hybrid approach to project management, which integrates elements of both traditional and agile methodologies, requires a careful examination of its advantages and disadvantages. This analysis is critical for making informed decisions about its implementation in various project environments. Organizations must weigh these factors to align their project management practices with their strategic goals and operational capabilities.

One of the primary benefits of the hybrid approach is its flexibility. By combining structured planning and adaptive processes, teams can respond swiftly to changes while maintaining a clear project roadmap. This flexibility is particularly valuable in dynamic industries where requirements frequently evolve. The structured component ensures that there is a coherent plan and timeline, while the agile elements allow for iterative development and continuous improvement. This duality can lead to enhanced project outcomes, as teams are not rigidly bound to a single methodology.

Another significant advantage is improved stakeholder engagement. The hybrid approach facilitates regular communication and feedback loops, which are hallmarks of agile practices. Stakeholders are kept informed and can provide input throughout the project lifecycle, leading to higher satisfaction and better alignment with business needs. Furthermore, the traditional aspects of the hybrid model, such as detailed documentation and predefined milestones, provide stakeholders with a sense of security and predictability.

However, the hybrid approach is not without its challenges. One of the main drawbacks is the complexity involved in integrating two distinct methodologies. Teams need to possess a deep understanding of both traditional and agile principles to effectively combine them. This requirement can lead to a steep learning curve and necessitate extensive training and development. Additionally, the dual approach can sometimes cause confusion or conflict within the team if not managed properly, as members might have differing preferences or levels of comfort with each methodology.

Resource allocation can also pose a challenge. The hybrid approach often demands more resources in terms of time, effort, and personnel compared to using a single methodology. Organizations must ensure they have the capacity to support this increased demand, which can be particularly taxing for smaller teams or projects with limited budgets. Effective resource management is crucial to prevent overburdening the team and to maintain project momentum.

Another potential downside is the risk of inconsistent implementation. Without clear guidelines and strong leadership, teams might struggle to balance the two methodologies effectively. This inconsistency can lead to fragmented processes, where neither the traditional nor the agile components are fully realized. To mitigate this risk, organizations should establish robust governance frameworks and provide continuous support to ensure that the hybrid approach is applied consistently across projects.

In terms of scalability, the hybrid approach may not be suitable for all types of projects. While it excels in environments that benefit from both structure and adaptability, it might be less effective for projects that require a highly specialized or purely linear approach. Organizations must carefully assess the nature of their projects and determine whether the hybrid model aligns with their specific needs and constraints.

The hybrid approach to project management offers a compelling blend of structure and flexibility, enhancing adaptability and stakeholder engagement. However, it also introduces complexity and resource challenges that must be carefully managed. By thoroughly evaluating these pros and cons, organizations can make strategic decisions about implementing hybrid methodologies, ensuring they maximize the benefits while mitigating potential drawbacks.

Making Informed Decisions

In the context of implementing hybrid approaches in project management, the capacity to make informed decisions is paramount. This subchapter delves into methodologies and frameworks that facilitate data-driven decision-making, ensuring that project managers can blend traditional and agile methodologies effectively.

Decision-making in hybrid project management necessitates a comprehensive understanding of both predictive and adaptive strategies. The integration of these methodologies requires a meticulous analysis of project variables, stakeholder expectations, and environmental conditions. A robust decision-making framework should incorporate quantitative data, qualitative insights, and predictive analytics to evaluate potential outcomes and risks.

One of the primary tools in making informed decisions is the Decision Support System (DSS). A DSS leverages data from various sources, including project management software, financial reports, and market analysis, to provide actionable insights. By utilizing algorithms and statistical models, a DSS can simulate different scenarios, allowing project managers to predict the impact of various decisions. This proactive approach helps in identifying potential bottlenecks and enables the formulation of contingency plans.

Additionally, the Analytical Hierarchy Process (AHP) is another critical method in decision-making. AHP assists in prioritizing tasks and resources by breaking down complex decisions into smaller, more manageable components. By comparing the relative importance of each element through pairwise comparisons, project managers can systematically evaluate the trade-offs involved. This structured approach ensures that decisions are aligned with the overall project goals and stakeholder priorities.

The integration of real-time data analytics is also essential. In a hybrid project environment, where changes can occur rapidly, the ability to access and analyze real-time data is crucial. Tools like dashboards and business intelligence software provide project managers with up-to-date information on project progress, resource allocation, and risk factors. By continuously monitoring key performance indicators (KPIs), project managers can make timely adjustments to their strategies, ensuring that the project remains on track.

Furthermore, the incorporation of machine learning algorithms enhances decision-making capabilities. Machine learning models can process vast amounts of data to identify patterns and trends that may not be immediately apparent to human analysts. These insights can inform decisions on resource allocation, timeline adjustments, and risk mitigation strategies. For instance, predictive maintenance algorithms can forecast equipment failures, allowing for preemptive measures that minimize downtime and cost overruns.

Stakeholder engagement is another critical aspect of informed decision-making. Regular communication with stakeholders ensures that their expectations and concerns are considered in the decision-making process. Techniques such as Delphi method, which involves iterative rounds of surveys to gather expert opinions, can be used to achieve consensus on critical decisions. This collaborative approach not only enhances the quality of decisions but also fosters stakeholder buy-in and support.

Risk management is integral to making informed decisions in hybrid projects. A thorough risk assessment, encompassing both qualitative and quantitative analysis, helps in identifying potential threats and opportunities. Techniques such as Monte Carlo simulations and sensitivity analysis provide insights into the probability and impact of various risks. By understanding the risk landscape, project managers can develop robust mitigation strategies and make decisions that balance risk and reward.

Incorporating these methodologies and tools into the decision-making process ensures that hybrid project management is both agile and structured. The ability to make informed decisions, backed by data and stakeholder input, enhances the likelihood of project success. By leveraging advanced analytics, stakeholder engagement, and risk management techniques, project managers can navigate the complexities of hybrid projects with confidence and precision.

Chapter 14: Future of Hybrid Project Management

Emerging Trends and Innovations

The landscape of project management is undergoing a significant transformation, driven by the integration of hybrid approaches that combine traditional methodologies with agile practices. This evolution is not merely a theoretical construct; it is being actively shaped by emerging trends and innovations that are redefining how projects are planned, executed, and delivered.

One of the most notable trends is the increasing emphasis on adaptability and flexibility. Traditional project management methodologies, such as Waterfall, have long been valued for their structured and sequential approach. However, the dynamic nature of today's business environments necessitates a more flexible framework. Agile methodologies, known for their iterative processes and responsiveness to change, are being integrated with traditional methods to form hybrid approaches that can better accommodate fluctuating project requirements and stakeholder expectations.

Technological advancements are playing a pivotal role in facilitating these hybrid approaches. The proliferation of project management software and tools that support both agile and traditional methodologies enables project managers to seamlessly transition between different phases of a project. These tools often come equipped with features such as real-time collaboration, automated reporting, and advanced analytics, which enhance the efficiency and effectiveness of project management practices. For instance, platforms like Jira and Trello, initially designed for agile projects, are now incorporating functionalities that cater to more structured project management needs, thereby fostering a more integrated approach.

Artificial Intelligence (AI) and machine learning are also making significant inroads into the realm of project management. These technologies are being leveraged to predict project outcomes, optimize resource allocation, and identify potential risks before they materialize. For example, AI-driven predictive analytics can analyze historical project data to forecast future project performance, allowing project managers to make more informed decisions. Machine learning algorithms can also assist in automating routine tasks, such as scheduling and progress tracking, thereby freeing up project managers to focus on more strategic aspects of the project.

The growing importance of stakeholder engagement and communication is another trend influencing the adoption of hybrid approaches. Effective communication is crucial for the success of any project, and hybrid methodologies offer a more holistic framework for stakeholder management. By combining the structured communication plans of traditional methodologies with the more frequent and informal interactions characteristic of agile practices, project managers can ensure that stakeholders are consistently informed and engaged throughout the project lifecycle. This integrated approach not only improves stakeholder satisfaction but also enhances the overall quality of the project deliverables.

Sustainability and social responsibility are increasingly becoming integral to project management practices. Organizations are recognizing the need to incorporate sustainable practices into their projects, and hybrid methodologies provide the flexibility to do so. For example, agile practices can be used to continuously assess and minimize the environmental impact of a project, while traditional methods can ensure that sustainability goals are systematically planned and monitored. This dual approach enables organizations to meet their sustainability objectives without compromising on project efficiency or quality.

In the context of organizational culture, the shift towards hybrid project management approaches is fostering a more collaborative and inclusive work environment. The amalgamation of agile and traditional methodologies encourages cross-functional teamwork and knowledge sharing, breaking down silos that often exist in traditional project settings. This cultural shift is not only enhancing team cohesion and morale but also driving innovation and creativity, as team members are empowered to contribute their unique perspectives and expertise.

The convergence of these emerging trends and innovations is ushering in a new era of project management, characterized by greater adaptability, technological integration, enhanced stakeholder engagement, and a commitment to sustainability. As organizations continue to navigate the complexities of modern project environments, the adoption of hybrid approaches will undoubtedly play a crucial role in their success.

Evolving Best Practices

The landscape of project management has undergone significant transformation, driven by the increasing complexity of projects and the rapid evolution of technological tools. The hybrid approach to project management, which integrates elements from both traditional and agile methodologies, has emerged as a compelling strategy to address these challenges. To optimize the implementation of this approach, it is imperative to continuously refine and adapt best practices based on empirical evidence and practical insights.

One of the fundamental principles in evolving best practices for a hybrid approach is the meticulous selection of methodologies that align with the unique requirements of a project. This involves a thorough assessment of the project's scope, objectives, stakeholder expectations, and resource constraints. For instance, a project with a well-defined scope and stable requirements may benefit from incorporating traditional waterfall elements for its planning and execution phases. Conversely, projects characterized by high levels of uncertainty and frequent changes may necessitate agile practices, such as iterative development and frequent stakeholder feedback loops.

Real-time data analytics and performance metrics play a crucial role in the continuous refinement of hybrid project management practices. By leveraging advanced analytics tools, project managers can gain valuable insights into project performance, identify bottlenecks, and make data-driven decisions to enhance efficiency. Key performance indicators (KPIs) such as project velocity, cycle time, and defect rates should be monitored rigorously to ensure that the hybrid approach is delivering the desired outcomes. Additionally, the use of predictive analytics can facilitate proactive risk management by forecasting potential issues and enabling timely interventions.

Effective communication and collaboration are also paramount in the successful implementation of a hybrid approach. Given the diverse methodologies involved, it is essential to foster a collaborative environment where team members are well-versed in both traditional and agile practices. Regular training sessions, workshops, and cross-functional meetings can help bridge knowledge gaps and ensure that all team members are aligned with the project's goals and methodologies. Moreover, the integration of collaborative tools such as project management software, instant messaging platforms, and virtual meeting solutions can enhance coordination and streamline workflows.

The role of leadership in evolving best practices cannot be overstated. Project leaders must demonstrate a deep understanding of both traditional and agile methodologies and possess the acumen to tailor these approaches to the specific needs of their projects. Leadership should also advocate for a culture of continuous improvement, encouraging team members to experiment with new techniques, share their experiences, and learn from both successes and failures. This iterative process of learning and adaptation is crucial for the ongoing evolution of best practices in hybrid project management.

Stakeholder engagement is another critical factor in refining hybrid project management practices. Regular interactions with stakeholders provide valuable feedback that can inform adjustments to the project plan and approach. Stakeholders should be involved in key decision-making processes and kept informed of project progress through transparent communication channels. This not only fosters trust and collaboration but also ensures that the project remains aligned with stakeholder expectations and delivers value.

In addition to these strategies, it is essential to document and disseminate best practices across the organization. Creating a centralized repository of lessons learned, case studies, and successful practices can serve as a valuable resource for future projects. This repository should be regularly updated and accessible to all team members, promoting a culture of knowledge sharing and continuous improvement.

The dynamic nature of project management necessitates an ongoing commitment to evolving best practices. By leveraging data analytics, fostering effective communication, demonstrating strong leadership, engaging stakeholders, and promoting knowledge sharing, organizations can optimize the implementation of hybrid project management approaches and achieve superior project outcomes.

The Role of Artificial Intelligence

Artificial intelligence (AI) has become a cornerstone in modern project management, offering a plethora of tools and methodologies that enhance the efficiency and effectiveness of hybrid project implementation. The integration of AI into project management frameworks not only automates routine tasks but also provides predictive analytics, decision-making support, and resource optimization.

AI-driven project management tools leverage machine learning algorithms to analyze historical data and identify patterns. These patterns can be instrumental in forecasting potential risks, estimating project timelines, and allocating resources more effectively. For instance, predictive analytics can identify bottlenecks before they occur, allowing project managers to take preemptive measures. This capability is particularly beneficial in hybrid projects, where the complexity of integrating traditional and agile methodologies can lead to unforeseen challenges.

Natural language processing (NLP) is another AI technology that has found significant applications in project management. NLP can automate the extraction of relevant information from project documents, emails, and meeting notes, thereby reducing the time and effort required for manual data entry and analysis. Additionally, NLP-powered chatbots can facilitate real-time communication and support, answering queries and providing updates to team members around the clock. This continuous availability ensures that project teams remain aligned and informed, irrespective of their geographical locations.

Resource management is another domain where AI excels. Machine learning algorithms can analyze the skills, availability, and workload of team members to optimize task assignments. This dynamic allocation not only maximizes productivity but also enhances team satisfaction by preventing burnout. Furthermore, AI can simulate various project scenarios to determine the most efficient resource allocation strategies, thereby enabling project managers to make data-driven decisions.

AI's role in enhancing decision-making processes cannot be overstated. Decision support systems (DSS) powered by AI can provide project managers with actionable insights derived from vast datasets. These systems can evaluate multiple variables, such as cost, time, and quality, to recommend the most viable course of action. The ability to process and analyze large volumes of data in real-time allows for more informed and timely decisions, which is crucial in the dynamic environment of hybrid projects.

Moreover, AI can significantly improve stakeholder engagement and satisfaction. Sentiment analysis tools can gauge stakeholder sentiments from communications and feedback, providing valuable insights into their concerns and expectations. This information can be used to tailor communication strategies and address issues proactively, thereby fostering a more collaborative and positive project environment.

The implementation of AI in project management also brings about ethical and governance considerations. Ensuring data privacy and security, maintaining transparency in AI-driven decisions, and addressing biases in algorithms are critical aspects that need to be managed. Establishing robust ethical guidelines and governance frameworks is essential to harness the full potential of AI while mitigating associated risks.

AI's transformative impact on hybrid project implementation is evident in its ability to automate routine tasks, provide predictive insights, optimize resources, and enhance decision-making processes. By leveraging AI technologies, project managers can navigate the complexities of hybrid projects more effectively, ensuring successful outcomes and delivering value to stakeholders.

Preparing for the Future

In the rapidly evolving landscape of project management, the integration of hybrid methodologies is not merely a trend but a necessity for future-proofing organizational practices. The fusion of traditional and agile approaches presents a robust framework, enabling teams to leverage the strengths of both methodologies to achieve optimal outcomes. This chapter delves into the strategic preparations necessary for organizations to effectively implement and sustain hybrid project management approaches, ensuring resilience and adaptability in the face of future challenges.

A critical component in preparing for the future is the establishment of a comprehensive training and development program. This program should be designed to enhance the skill sets of project managers and team members, equipping them with the necessary competencies to navigate the complexities of hybrid methodologies. Training modules should encompass both theoretical knowledge and practical applications, providing a balanced approach to learning. By fostering a culture of continuous improvement and learning, organizations can ensure that their workforce remains adept at utilizing hybrid strategies effectively.

Technological infrastructure plays a pivotal role in the successful implementation of hybrid project management. Investing in advanced project management tools and software that support hybrid frameworks is essential. These tools should facilitate seamless integration, real-time collaboration, and adaptive planning. The selection of technology should be guided by the specific needs of the organization, ensuring that it aligns with the existing processes and enhances overall efficiency. Robust data analytics capabilities are also crucial, enabling teams to make informed decisions based on real-time insights and performance metrics.

Organizational alignment and stakeholder engagement are fundamental to the successful adoption of hybrid methodologies. It is imperative to foster a shared vision and understanding of the hybrid approach across all levels of the organization. This can be achieved through clear communication, transparent processes, and inclusive decision-making. Engaging stakeholders early in the transition process and maintaining continuous dialogue helps in managing expectations and securing buy-in. Organizational policies and governance structures should be adapted to support the hybrid model, ensuring alignment with strategic objectives and operational practices.

Risk management is another critical aspect that must be addressed in preparing for the future. Hybrid project management inherently involves a degree of uncertainty due to the dynamic nature of combining different methodologies.

Developing a robust risk management framework that anticipates potential challenges and outlines mitigation strategies is essential. This framework should be dynamic, allowing for regular updates and adjustments based on project progress and emerging risks. By proactively managing risks, organizations can safeguard against disruptions and ensure the smooth execution of hybrid projects.

The human element cannot be overlooked in the transition to hybrid project management. Cultivating a culture that embraces change and innovation is vital. Leadership plays a crucial role in this regard, setting the tone for an adaptive and resilient organizational mindset. Leaders should exemplify the principles of hybrid project management, fostering an environment that encourages experimentation, agility, and collaboration. Recognizing and rewarding efforts that contribute to the successful implementation of hybrid methodologies can further reinforce positive behaviors and drive sustained commitment.

In conclusion, preparing for the future in the context of hybrid project management necessitates a multifaceted approach. By investing in training, technology, organizational alignment, risk management, and cultural transformation, organizations can position themselves to not only adapt to but thrive in the evolving project management landscape. The ability to seamlessly integrate traditional and agile methodologies will be a critical determinant of success, enabling organizations to deliver value consistently and efficiently in an increasingly complex world.

www.ingramcontent.com/pod-product-compliance
Lightning Source LLC
Chambersburg PA
CBHW071918210526
45479CB00002B/466